Poems Purely for Pleasure

A Lifetime Collection of Original Poems and Songs

Raymond W. Groves

VANTAGE PRESS
New York / Los Angeles / Chicago

To my wife,
my brothers and sisters,
and my friends,
without whose encouragement and insistence
this book would never have been published

FIRST EDITION

All rights reserved, including the right of
reproduction in whole or in part in any form.

Copyright © 1989 by Raymond W. Groves

Published by Vantage Press, Inc.
516 West 34th Street, New York, New York 10001

Manufactured in the United States of America
ISBN: 0-533-01835-1

Library of Congress Catalog Card No.: 88-91284

Contents

Introduction xiii
Part I. On the Family Farm
  September Morn 3
  September Escapade 3
  Arboreal Gratitude 4
  Teenager's Dilemma 4
  Reflection while Digging
    Potatoes 4
  Hang in There, You Little
    Folks 5
  Bugger 5
  Don't We All 6
  The Bright Side 6
  Firefly 6
  Contentment 7
  Life 7
  Pessimistic Prognosis 8
  Successful Hunt 9
  Roughing It 9
  Take Your Pick! 10
  Cherry-Pickers, All 11
Part II. In Military Service
  I Want to Be 15
  Whip-poor-will 15
  Bivouac 16
  Arkansas 17
  Mortar Mishap 17
  Pacific? 18
  Manila, P.I. 19
  Stars 19
  Mirage a la Manila 20
  Tropical Weather 22
  Whose Hue? 23
  Fidelity 23
  Stopping on a Tropical
    Evening 24
  Otegoan? 24
  A Legacy 25
  Minor Misery 26
  Dental Uhg Glug Blub 26
  Impromptu Operation 27
  Complaint 27
  To Jim, a Mechanic 28
  Philosophic Brevities 28
  Plain Geometry 29
  Chicago 32
  Friend in the
    Philippines 32
  No Favorite Flavor 33
  Manilha 33
  Sunrise-Sunset 34
  Overseas Time 34
  USAT *Admiral Hughes* 35
  Golden Gate 35
  Troop Train 35
Part III. The Ladies
  An International Beauty 39
  Esther 39
  Sue 40
  Alice 40
  Mom 41
  Inez 42
  Hurry Back Anyway,
    Hon 42
  Gift List—for Inez 42
  PS: Comic Sequel 43
  Mandy 43
  Daughter-in-Law 43
  Carol I 44
  Carol II 44
  Mary, Dental Hygienist
    par Excellence 45

Appreciation	45	Thank You	61
Welcome, Meara Ann	46	Happy Birthday	61
Elaine	47	Heart Felt	62
Melissa	47	Love Me Now	62
Sew What? Sue	47	We Love Her	63
Queen Susan	48	Pagan Mug Song	63
Sweet Sue	48	November Nocturne	64
Glenda	49	An All-Holiday Wish	64
Fiction, Fun, and Fantasy, Together with Some Poetry	49	Pinned	65
		Jumper	65
October Fantasy	50	Young Love	66
Mary	50	Valentine II	66
Agnes, Citizen of the Year	51	Disappointed	66
		Love Changes	67
Elma	52	Birthday = ?	68
Saint Patrick's Day	52	Good-Luck Charm	68
Erin Go Bragh	53	Loved One	69
I'm a Regular United Nations, but—This Is Saint Patrick's Day	53	All My Love	70
		Togetherness	70
		Love Poem	70
Irish Lass	54	Love Poem II	71
Lovely Lady from Down Under	54	More Love Poems	71
		Ever Together	72
The Saga of the Sage and the Sagittarians	55	Hurry Back Again	73
		Alone	73
Part IV. Love		Lonely	74
Love Is New	59	December 16 Birthday	74
Let's Face It—It's Bigger than Both of Us or We're Young and Can Afford to Wait or Let's Wait for Something More Permanent on a Trial Basis	60	In Defense of Separate Vacations	75
		Think Happy	75
		Misnomer	76
		Independence Day	76
		Longing	77
		Lonely II	77
Love Impossible	60	Together Forever	78
Valentine	61	Signs of Spring	78
		It Happens	79

I Care	79
Longing and Waiting	80
I'll Love You More	81
Honey, I Love You Enough	82
Short Sweet Memories	82
Sixty-five Approacheth	83
Remembering	83
I'd Love to Share	84
Mind Full of You	84
Between the Lines	85
Lobelia and Me	85
Homebody	86
Eyeful Power	86
A Christmas Love	87
Christmas Loving	87
Élan	88
Anniversary	88
It Happens Every Time	89
Blossoms All	89
Baby, I'll Be There	90
Uninvolved	90
Bound to Be Free	91
Mother's Day (Out)	91
Part V. Grandchildren	
Grandchildren	95
Thoughts on Growing Up	95
Grandad	96
Vocation?	97
Moist and Misty	97
Strange Bedfellow	98
April Foolishness	99
Classroom Crisis	100
Linguistically Speaking	101
Broke It, Huh?	101
Lucky Break	102
Here's a Mouthful	102
Eskimo Economics	103
Parapooch	104
Fish Story	106
Part VI. Battle of the Sexes	
For Men Only	111
The Imperfect Man	111
Poor Shopper	112
Filing Singly or Jointly?	112
When She Sends You Shopping	113
Composite Compulsive Cleaner	114
Cleanliness and Godliness?	116
Rules of Rhyme	117
Wordy	117
Strike Three—Y'er Out!	118
Loser	119
By Choice	120
Feminine Mystique	121
I Had This Dream	122
Passes Are Passé	122
The Rock	123
Cool Kiss	123
This Bugs Me	124
Odds	125
When the Honeymoon Is Over	126
Travel Talk	127
One Phone Call?	128
The Winner	129
Be Prepared	129
Because	130

Bedtime Story	130
Marital Semi-Bliss	131
Helpmates	132
The Storyteller	133
Seems Like Forever	134
Hear, Hear!	135
One Never Knows	135
Advice to Single Ladies	136
My Keeper	137
Caution—No Lock!	137
Singles-Bar Encounter	138
Fire Extinguisher (Gift)	138
Nuts to ———	139
Social Standing	139
Yuppie	140
"Never Mind, I'll Do It Myself"	141
She'd Better Not	141

Part VII. Philosophy—Religion—the Church

Partners	145
Late Spring Snow	146
Harbinger	146
Snow Job	147
Piddle Paddle	147
Versatile Love	148
The Censors	149
Let's Not Forget	150
Lay Leader? You've Got to Be Kidding!	151
Tongue-in-Cheek Organ Fund Plea or Who's Gonna Pay so the Organ Can Play?	152
Organ Fund Plea	153
Don't Count Me Out, Lord	154
Healthy, Wealthy, and Wise	155
On Reincarnation	156
The Malpractice Suers	157
Speaking of Words	158
Seldom Pray-er	158
"For Whom the Bell Tolls"	159
With Love	160
Gardening	161
Forest Cathedral	161
Destiny	162
Aquatic Flight	162
Reverend Dodson	163
Seven Best Buys	164
Ordinary People	165
Retiring Church Organist	166
The Bridge Builder	167
The Apprentice	168
Hot and Cold	169
Sequel to "Hot and Cold"	169
Christmas Reflections	170
Gift List—for My Friends	171
Christmas Spirit	171
Just Naturally Neighborly	172
An Offertory Parody: How Long Has It Been?	172
Biblical Logic	173
To a Beloved Pastor and Family	173
A Weak Sinner's Prayer for Strength	174
Let's Face It	174

Think about It	175
One Man Awake	175
One Man Awake Parody	176
Oh, My Soul and Body	177
Reincar-notion?	177
Garden Story	178
Another Garden Story	178
Fitting Footwear	179
Between Anthems	179
How Do I Remember My Age?	180
Recipe for One Small Choir	180

Part VIII. Love Songs and a Few Others

My Love Songs	183
Long, Long Ago	184
Good-bye, My Lover, Good-bye	185
I Love You Just the Same	187
Windchill Loving	188
Baby, What Am I Supposed to Do?	189
Think	190
Love's Memories	191
Just Five Years	192
The Good Old Days	193
So Beautiful	194
Your Nose Is Itchin'	195
Sweet Gift	196
I'm Gonna See My Baby	197
I Want to Wake Up	198
'Cause It's True	199
Love Is for the Living	200
Need You Near Me	201
My Songs	202
Finders Keepers	203
Love Came Late	204
I Need You	205
What'll I Do?	206
Christmas Lonely	207
Whole Lot o' Woman	208
Sorry	209
She'd Make a Bulldog Break His Chain	210
Forgetting	211
Moonlight Skate	212
I Lied	213
Alone	213
You Stayed Away Too Long	214
Home with You	215
While You Were Away	216
I'm Your Baby	217
Love	218
Sweet Licks	219
Double Love	220
The Streak	222
Lonely but Hopeful	223
The Lonesome Game	223
My Baby That Was	224
Night Light (or Energy Crisis)	225
Just a Common Pup	226
Queen Loretta	227
Empty Cookie Jar	228
Summer's Gone	229
———	231
My Modern Verse	232
Gordy's Song	233

Part IX. Travel

My Little Map Reader and Me	237

Broad-minded	237	Un-Success Story	260
Grand Canyon	238	Unemployed	261
Ocean Lover's Observation	238	SOB	262
		First-Class Male	263
New Mexico	239	To All Postal Employees	264
Haiti	239		
Dependable Dawn	240	Please Write	264
Solitary Whale	240	Super's Shorthanded Lament	265
Queen Elizabeth II Crisis	241		
		The Day before Christmas	266
A Thank You	241		
Oceans	242	Postal Retirement	267
Caribbean Clouds	242	Part XI. Potpourri	
A Memory of Cape Cod	243	Food for Thought	271
		The Bright Side	271
Maine—First Impressions	243	Color Preference	271
		Unbreakable	271
Senior Hot Rods	244	Technology Is Wonderful	272
Close Encounter	245		
Halifax	246	Rubik's Cube	272
Millie's Micmacs Tour	247	With My Bare Face Hanging Out	273
	247		
Nova Scotia Tour	248	Listen—Ye Shall Hear	273
Cabot's Trail	250	Woods Lover	273
Where the Heart Is	251	Addicted	274
Home Again	251	Financial Propanity	274
Virginia Tour	252	You Over There	275
Easy Does It	252	Who *Mis*names These Things?	276
Williamsburg, Virginia	253		
McAdoo, Pennsylvania	254	Language Barrier	276
		Must It *b*?	277
Claudia and Jackie	254	Sure Thing	277
Part X. Economics— Politics—Taxes		Play on Words	278
		Of Animal (and Human) Behavior	278
Taxpayer's Lament or Taxing Us to Death	257		
		Permanent?	278
"Fixed" Income	258	Waiter?	278
Political Poverty	259	Compatible	278

In Defense of Small Strawberries	280
Phony Greeter	280
A Day That Will Live?	281
Soul-Searching Study	281
Early Lesson	282
Rheum for Improvement	282
Age-old Question	282
Perfect Gift	283
Electric Eel	283
Choir Director	284
Synonym	284
Grand Larceny?	285
A Modern Youth	285
Pal-in-drome	286
A Typical Typist	286
A Gender Gem	287
The Weather Guessers	287
Whale-Watch Tour	288
Anni	288
Susquehanna Chorus (1988)	289
Jenny Kissed Me	290
Home with Mary	290
What! Already?	291
Since Time Began	291
A Fitting End	292
That's Me, All Right	292
Success Story	293
The Worm Turns	294
Now I Remember	295
From Ay to Aye	295
Horsepital Report	296
Modern-Day Shaker	296
Clapp Trap	296
Greenhouse Absentee	297
Man-to-Plant Monologue	297
Gift Wrap	297
Re-probate	298
Crime of the Month	298
On Hypnosis	298
Happy Holidays	299
A Man for All Seasons	299
Violence in the Garden	300
Down and In	300
Dietary Preference?	301
Greenhouse Plants and People	301
On Ambidexterity	302
Let It Ring	302
Western Square Dance Class	303
Sheba	304
For a Ceramic Frog	304
Energy Crisis	305
Ain't Technology Grand?	306
Enigma	306
It's in There	307
Hermit	307
Condiment	308
On Three-Letter Nonwords	308
Portrait of a Jogger	309
Another Bridge Builder	309
Nothing to Sneeze At	310
Heir Apparent	310
Apology	311
Poetic Brevity	311
A Fine Line	312
On Self-Deprecation	312
Happy Medium	313
Hospitalized Again?	313

A Friend's Hemorrhoid Surgery	313
Expensive Care	314
Donor or Donee?	314
Reluctant Patient	314
It Only Hurts . . .	315
Surgery	315
Get Well Soon	316
Minor Surgery	317
Daylight Saving Time	317
Blue	318
Sequel to "Blue"	319
Pen Pal	319
Ambition	320
Belle	320
Housewarming	320
Driving Instruction	321
Floaters	321
To a Dog-Bitten Friend	321
Key Man	322
"Where's the Beef?"	322
Dodger-Mania	322
Odd Fellow	323
March Seventeenth	323
Hostess	323
Unsolicited Wake-Up	323
Pen-cil Pal	324
Delayed Grand Opening	324
The Critic	324
Compuslive Rhymer	325
Just a Few More Limericks	325
Heller	325
. . . "and Touch Someone"	325
Shoofly Pie	326
On the Briny Deep	326
Jough Blough?	326
Bush	326
Father's Day Is Forever	327
Political Observation	327

Part XII. Somewhat Personal

Character	331
What's for Fun?	331
Life-Style	332
As Is	332
Advice	333
Appearances	333
By Comparison	334
Roots	334
Ancestry and Destiny	335
Nature Lore	336
September Song	336
The Trouble Is	337
Siblings	337
Relatively Speaking	337
She Can't Understand It	338
Sibling Rivalry? Not Us!	338
RSVP	339
Seventy-five Years Ago: My Brother, Ted	339
It Takes One to Know One	340
Bob I	340
Bob II	341
Brotherly Greetings	341
Brotherly Christmas Greetings	341
Family Get-together	342

Higher Education	342
Firstborn	343
Shadows	344
One Name for Four Sons	345
The Children's Rowr	346
Unwritten Book	346
To a Grandson Born on Christmas Eve	347
Aaron—Plus One	347
Gift List	348
For a Friend	348
Family	348
Young Bill	349
Young Graduate	349
Graduation Gift	350
Paperboy	350
To Neglected Friends	351
A Grandad's Dilemma	351
Sorry Situation	351
Logic to Live By	352
Autobiography in a Nutshell	353
Occupational Hazards	355
Postal Problem	356
To Friends Departing	357
To a Friend	358
Farewell to Special Friends	359
Special Friends' Special Anniversary	359
Good-bye to Good Friends	360
Chosen	360
Donor's Prayer	361
Blood Bank Deposit	361
Preteaching Reflections of a Volunteer Reading Tutor	362
Five Gifts	362
Bean Burner	363
Motorcycling	364
My Alibi	364
The Class of '34	365
Class Reunion	366
Harmonic Convergence?	367
Unlikely Listener	367
Nate-urally	367
Fringe Benefit	368
Things I Believe	368
On Selling the Grange	369
Old Timer's Olympics	370
Runner	371
Not to Worry	371
We'll Never Get Out of Here Alive or I'll Go Quietly	372
Unemployed	373
Final Curtain	374
Finally, Freedom	375
Reassessing Retirement	375
Uncommon Sense	376
Waiting Again	377
Versatile Verse-a-Pile	378
A Man of All Seasons	378
The Time Is Coming	379
Last Rights	379
Premonition	380
Swan Song	381
I'll Go—but Not Voluntarily	382

Part XIII. More Truth than Poetry

Who Is Poor?	385
Parable of a Strike	386
Portrait of a Failure	387
Retirement: Sugar-coated Unemployment	388
Memories of Youth	388
Homelife Vignette	389
Judicial Decision	389
Words of Wisdom and Advice to Young Friends	389
Crisis Communiqué	390
Wedding Vows	391
Pessimist's Minisermon	392
Grains of Truth: The Gleanings of a Lifetime	393
Exerpts from Grove's Laws	395

Introduction

"An artist is the one thing a man can claim he is and nobody can prove he isn't." Thus said Will Rogers, one of America's best-loved, homespun philosphers and humorists. My contention is that poets are artists who work with pen and words instead of brush and oils and as such are entitled to that same artistic immunity.

A poet's work must necessarily reflect his upbringing, experiences, and environment; it is, of necessity, somewhat autobiographical. But then sometimes imagination and fantasy take control, and pure fiction-in-rhyme emerges, as many diverse subjects fall prey to the prolific pen. The reader may judge in which category a given poem falls.

My earliest recollection of writing a poem was when I was in the sixth or seventh grade. It was written in conclusion of a brief autobiography titled "I." At that time I had no vision of starting a collection of original verse, so that the very first one was lost—except for the final two lines, which I recall from memory . . .

And if you think these lines are something of a joke
Remember—I am but the nut that may someday be an oak.

Part I

On the Family Farm

The next several poems emerged at a time in which I was working on the family farm, during and after my high school years. It was not a particularly productive period, but after all, I was working.

(Inspired by a scene on a neighboring farm while on my Sunday morning paper route.)

September Morn

The sun broke through the mist and fog
And surprised a clump of goldenrod
Bending over a farmer's pond
To drink—and offer thanks to God.

September Escapade

Smooth white bodies, round and firm
Were lying naked in the sun
Lying, waiting on the ground
Waiting for the hand of one
Whose swift grasp would clutch and claim them
One brief moment, all possessed—
While blue skies and breezes witness
Each is wanted, each caressed.
Yet no thought of sin or evil
Mars the sweet, bright interim
And the farm lad whistles gaily
—Bringing the potatoes in.

Arboreal Gratitude

Our thanks for all the trees that bring
Fruit in autumn—
Blossoms and shade in spring,
A canopy for woodflowers sweet
That cling together, and for our feet
A thick soft carpet of leaves long gone to rest.
For boughs where birds may nest
Safe from intrusion—
And special thanks for philanthropic maples
Annual donors for a sap transfusion.

Teenager's Dilemma

Of what use is youth
When truth is concealed from youthful eyes
—We'll be old before we're wise.

Reflection while Digging Potatoes

If we graded people just like potatoes
By the way they appeared on the scene
I'd have been discarded long before high school
—For I was both little *and* green.

Hang In There, You Little Folks

I was such a tiny baby
And I grew up feeling small,
Knowing I would never be
Like some others—BIG and TALL

I was small in kindergarten
I was small in grammar school
Still, my size did not deter me
From becoming quite a fool.

I went all the way through high school
Mature growth had never come
But the year after graduation
—I gruesome.

Bugger

I have to "bug" the potatoes
Or fail to have a crop—
It's been left to me to see
That those bugs don't eat the top.

But toiling long, all bowed and bent
I perceive through misery
I don't bug them half as much
As *they* are "bugging" me.

Don't We All

The p'tato bug is oh, so brave
He won't run his soul to save
He won't fight back to save his hide
But he ends up either dead—or died.

The Bright Side

I thought he was a firefly
But fireflies light up at night
And here we were in broad daylight
—He wouldn't even try.

He flipped—I saw the bulb so pale
And knew the coming darkness
He'd illuminate with sparkness
Of the phosphorescence underneath his tail.

Firefly

The industry, the zeal that men display
Has often been compared to that of ants
That strive and strive 'gainst massive loads in vain
—I think that many people are more like fireflies
With their greatest talent farthest from their brain.

Contentment

"Man wants but little here below."
The words once written long ago
Are just as true, or more today.
We only want—
A chance to work, to serve mankind or
To produce a useful item, thus to find
The self-respect, the peace of mind
Of knowing the task's well done;
Enough to eat, good health for all of mine
A place to lay our heads, and carefree sleep
To make us new, to greet the dawn with zest
To run the course with neither shame nor fear.
These things to have will make us truly blest;
What more to have would make us happier here?

Life

Life is like this little verse
With neither rhyme nor reason to it
Yet they both could be much worse
So grin and bear and struggle through it.

Pessimistic Prognosis

The planting season's in full swing
And every insect that can sting
Or bite or chew or bore a hole
Is determined to meet his destruction goal.

A dozen weeds will start to grow
Where one weed grew before;
There'll be a hundred different kinds
And forty-'leven more.

For every crop we plan to raise
There'll be a dozen germs to fight
Like smut and rust and club root
And damping off and blight.

The weatherman's against us, too
In spite of all our praying;
We'll have sunshine when we need it wet
But we'll have lots of rain, you bet
In harvest and in haying.

All these problems don't scare us
We've solved *one* tough equation
We know exactly where we'll spend
Our annual summer vacation.

Successful Hunt

I didn't shoot a buck this year
And yet I count my hunt a fine success.
I had two days of stealing through the woods
—My hunting was among the very best
I've ever done.

I saw a fox go slinking by with backward glance
And heard the wind, sweet music, whispering;
Watched the clinging leaves' mad, shivering dance;
Saw a squirrel perform his daring leap
Through space from tree to tree;
And watched five deer seek haven
From hunters and the storm
—And none of them saw me.

Roughing It

Roughing it? You call that rough?
With all that highfalutin' stuff?
A fancy cabin, fine food to eat
Electric razor, gasoline heat
An air mattress and folding cot—
It seems to me, my friend, you've got
All the comforts of home.

To me, to "rough it" means a tent
With beans or pancakes, a woodstove's scent,
A bed of boughs with blankets spread,
A week-old beard in the razor's stead;
For cooking, ancient battered kettles,
For toilet paper, a handful of nettles.
Brother, I mean—THAT'S ROUGH!

Take Your Pick!

Some birds and I have a cherry tree—
(I only wanted my share)
But there were a whole lot more of them
And they didn't really care
If I got enough for a pie or not.

They all kept picking and picking a lot—
Not one would dig worms
As a good robin should
Those lazy birds were just no good;
No longer they'd work for honest pay
But drank cherry wine in the tree all day.

To make matters worse
And me madder and madder
Those doggone robins were
—Using my ladder!

Cherry-Pickers, All

I talk to the birds, but they don't care
They won't give up and they won't scare.
"This cherry-thievin' has got to stop
You've had your share, right off the top.
You didn't think I could get that high?
You know that line's an outright lie
Pure poppycock and brazen bull—
You birds just wanted your gullets full.
Furthermore, I trimmed that tree—
All you trim is the fruit and me.
Then, too, I also fertilized
With the best ingredients yet devised
—The fertilizer that you put out
Is the sort of mess we can do without.
Get your feathered fannies far away
Find an early worm or a bug a day;
Consider the cherry-picking 'quits'
'Cause *I* want more than just the pits."

Part II

In Military Service

Military service was a very special experience for me. As for many, it represented a fork in life's path that changed my life. Again, it was a very busy time with not much time for writing. Still, an occasional poem reared its head and was recorded. One such poem is "I Want to Be," which deals with being away from home for the first time; some might call it "homesickness."

Part II

Military Service

I Want to Be

Where the April sun is beating on a peaceful little town
And the fleecy clouds lie sleepy in the sky
You can hear a church bell ringing
And an oriole is singing, as
A lumbering bumblebee goes grumbling by.

There are blossoms small and sweet
In the carpet at your feet
They are scattered like the evening sky is starred;
That's where I want to be
And they're waiting there for me
Back in my own backyard.

Whip-poor-will

Nocturnal song so sad and shrill
Is sung by Willie Whip-poor-will
Shrieking through the silence deep
Disrupting thoughts, dispelling sleep;
Of all the songs I've ever heard
I'd rather never hear the bird
In fact if it were up to me
I'd whip-poor-will unmercifully.

Bivouac

They told us bivouac was tough
A couple of days would be enough
To make us wish we'd never heard
That often-cussed, much-hated word.
But now we've been on bivouac
We know just what it's like
The way it starts, you roll a pack
And then you take a hike;
Midst nature's camouflage, the shade
A canvas village soon is made
For meals, the chow truck rolls around
For beds, four blankets on the ground.
We hide and seek from tree to tree
To learn the lessons of the infantry;
So what the heck's the fuss about?
Two pleasant weeks of camping out!

Arkansas

Arkansas is wonderful
In fair or stormy weather;
Sunshine and dust, the rain and mud
Always pair together.

Arkansas is marvelous
The climate here is dual;
When the sun's not blazing hot
It's raining here on you-all.

Though Arkansas is beautiful
As viewed from basic training;
It's always dusty when it's fair
And muddy when it's raining.

Mortar Mishap

We set our mortars on the line
Our practice rounds to spend
The sergeant stooped too close to mine
He's mortarfied—no end.

Pacific?

Who named the Pacific, "pacific"
Must have been someone who didn't know
That the waves out here are terrific
And the winds never cease to blow.
There is no peace for the ocean—
Wearing a worried frown
With a restless frenzied motion
It wanders hither and yon, helplessly up and down.
The very air is ill at ease
It has no home nor place to rest
No sunny meadow or friendly wood
On the crest of a gentle slope;
But like a sullen, thwarted villain
Exiled and divested of all hope
Overcome, at once, by anger and dejections
Springs on a fiery charger and rides off in all directions.
"Lonesone," "restless," "tempestuous," or "vast"
Are appellations fitting of your fame;
So let's dismiss misnomers of the past
"Pacific"—I suggest you change your name.

Manila, P.I.

Crippled city, victim of modern war
Crumbled buildings, shattered streets
Are monuments to armies gone before;
But sadder still are shattered souls
Ruined lives that yet go on and on
Seeking pitiful existence midst shell holes,
Ashes, and utter destruction . . .

Crippled city, far less difficult
Your task of reconstruction
Than to fill your people's greatest needs
—Resurrection of their morals
—Indoctrination to a creed.

Stars*

The stars are friends
To all the guards
Who spend the lonely night
In silent vigil.
The moon may shed
A ghastly light
Enough but to betray;
But stars are pins
That hold aloft
The canopy of night
—Until the day.

*Inspired while on solitary guard duty atop a wall of old Fort Santiago in Manila, 1946.

Mirage a la Manila

If you've never been far away from home
In a country and climate that are not your own
You'd never believe the thoughts that come to mind
For no other reason than to kind of relieve
The ache that's in the heart or to cause
The sweet sadness that memories impart.
Thoughts can't be imprisoned on islands small
Or like people, be thwarted by a puny wall
But they soar o'er the deep like a bird on the wing
And return with memories of anything.
Though it's many a day and I'm far away
From the land where they belong
A supersonic hearing aid
Recaptures the lilting, ever-haunting
Maytime oriole's song.
As I crouch and stare across wasteland bare
A trick of the sight to my utter delight
Unfolds a field of blossoming clover
Watched over by bobolink guards
From posts atop the wry sour dock
And a brazen 'chuck a pose has struck
By his fortress 'neath a rock.

The tropical sun can't melt the snow
That I enjoyed two years ago
And the ice on the pond that knew the bite
Of reckless skates in the clear moonlight
Like a frozen sheet appears impervious to the broiling heat.
Where seasons mean nought but sun or rain,
A mental album opens to a scene of wooded hills:
Leaves splashed with brilliant crimson stain;
Yellow fields wearing the crew cut
Of grain that's gone to mills;
Brown cornfields waiting patiently
The husker's horny hand;
Blue skies, October sunshine
A picture Nature planned.

These things I've seen and felt and heard
All memories that were conjured up
Like dreams, from pleasures I once knew
—And long to know again.

Tropical Weather

There's a factory in the tropics
Where the weather all is made;
By giant mixers it is stirred
By giant fetters stayed.

The weather maker does his worst
With what he has on hand
To make things inconvenient
And spoil what you have planned.

Three variation may he use
His choices are erratic;
The broiling heat, he need not choose
The *heat* is automatic.

For variation from the heat
He has the pouring rain;
He drops it earthward in a sheet
Turns it off—then on again.

Weary of these, should he grow
Thoughtless, as a drunk baboon
He thunders "Joe, I think I'll blow"
As he pulls the lever labeled EMERGENCY TYPHOON.

So tropical weather, all in all
Is mighty hard to take;
I'd trade it all to watch the fall
Majestic, of *one* parachuting snowflake.

Whose Hue?

High over Luzon's lofty clouds
A rainbow spanned the sky
One end anchored deep in a rice paddy
The other, far beyond my eye.

Whence came those hues so delicate
So dainty and so varied?
Where else were tints, so expertly
So gently blended, sweetly married?

And then I knew, to what far spot
That iridescent archway led—
The other end could only be
In Mother's sweet pea bed.

Fidelity

She promised when they parted at the station
That her heart forever would be true
While he was in the service of the nation
In a country far away across the blue.

The years went by—first one, then two
Arriving home, her sweetheart was dismayed
To learn that though her *heart* was true
The rest of her had up and gone and strayed.

Stopping on a Tropical Evening
(With apologies to Robert Frost.)

Whose girl this is, I do not know
I would not care to meet him though
I'm sure that it would give him pain
To see her set my heart aglow.

My little jeep must think it queer
To find a female sitting here
He knows that she is not GI
And I'll have more to do than steer.

He gives a snort of mild disdain
A muffled, muttered, "What, again?"
And then as by telepathy
He purrs into a lonely lane.

The girl is lovely, sweet, and dark
The night holds promise of a lark
I'll not drive far before I park
I'll not drive far before I park.

Otegoan?

There was a young man from Otego
Who once did far over the sea go
But he said, and I quote,
"I'm a born Otegoat—
No more travel for me, my amigo."

A Legacy

No monetary wealth have I
Nor will I have the day I die;
So sons of mine themselves may gain
What'er they seek in life, and learn
That not the goal they do attain
But the struggle and the strife
Of winning it affords the thrill
The pleasure and the joy
That crowns success.

Instead, I'll leave a mountain peak
Their gaze to hold enraptured;
The soft caress on sunburned cheek
Of breezes soft; the never-captured
Splendor of the sunset; the hoarfrost
And the crunch of frozen snow;
For music of every kind, a love
Including the sweetly plaintive whistle of
The woodchuck and the husky whisper of the pines;

Abounding health and strength of mind
These and all the others wonders
Of Nature to enjoy, They'll find
A richness of life in these daily pleasures
And loving them will have enough of treasures
Though fame and fortune pass them by.
Contentment, peace, and happiness be theirs
And when these fail to bring delight
Then, likewise, may they leave them to *their* heirs
As rosy dawn succeeds the stygian night.

Minor Misery

If it ever should fall to your lot to be
In a hospital when you're not
Almost dead, your leg's not torn off at the knee
A terrible pain doesn't screech through your brain
Your inwards don't writhe and strain
You're not very sick, you'll get well real quick;
Then, Brother, take it from me
Than death, there's a fate worse, a horrible curse
A hospital patient to be
—Yet ignored by the beautiful nurse.

Dental Uhg Glug Blub

Among the things that puzzle me
And ever are a mystery
I find this most amazing.

That doctors, though of high esteem
And knowledge vast, can never seem
To realize this simple truth:

When the mouth is opened wide
With tools and paddles propped inside
—To answer questions is uncouth.

Impromptu Operation

She'd had a tonsillectomy
And then an appendectomy
But when she had an auto wreck
The windshield scalpeled off her neck.
Doctors came for miles to see
—Her nifty nectilectomy.

Complaint

Against the army, I've a gripe
It's one that can't be cured
It's not the food, another stripe
Or any of the usual tripe
           BUT
I've met and known so many friends
Since I've been in the service
We part and then our friendships end
—We never meet again.

To Jim, a Mechanic

When the starter is locked or the thing won't go
The oil lines broken or the gas won't flow
The carburetor's gummy or a tire is flat
The enficle drum has a broken slat
The gallopin' rod is running hot
And instead of a nibblin' pin, it's not
The spiliken wheel has a broken spoke
The gas tank's fouled with rum and coke
In short, it the thing's not up to par
Hold it, Bud, right where you are—
Just call that guy with the greasy clothes
There's grease in his ears and on his nose;
On his face is a grin, in his hand a tool
He's the kid that works in the motor pool.

Philosophic Brevities

A philosopher and poet
Though my features scarely show it
That I am and that I will remain

My rhyme and wit I'll pour on
Though my friends may call me "moron"
I don't mind because I know that they're insane.

Plain Geometry

One and one make two
Speaking arithmetically
But speaking biologically
—One and one make three.

* * * *

I've traveled many miles away
Had many homes—and yet
None were there that I cared to stay
Nor left without regret.

* * * *

All men are created equal
We've been told, but here is a sequel
—Women were created then
For making monkeys out of men.

* * * *

To your friends tell not your troubles
Lest you be to them a bore
—Tell them to your enemies
They'll enjoy them *so* much more.

Though I don't own a camera or a Kodak
When I go home, I know I'll go back
With pictures of places and things I've seen
That I can flash on my mental screen.
My buddies had eyes but did not see
—They were taking pictures so frantically.

✻ ✻ ✻ ✻

I've had a lot of troubles that are mighty sad to hear
But now stark tragedy has struck and stood me on my ear
I've lost the very dearest friend a man could ever lose
He ran off with my wife last week
—I miss *him* like the deuce.

✻ ✻ ✻ ✻

I saw a sign upon a door
It said just LADIES, nothing more
I oped the door and ventured in
The language I heard was a sin
So now I pen these lyric lines
To say—I don't believe in signs.

✻ ✻ ✻ ✻

I have a brother-in-law named Tom
Who helped with the a-tom-ic bomb
Filled with conceit from toe to brim
—He thinks they named it after *him*.

Thoughts and ideals should be kept very high
Along with all valuable stuff
—Very few people will stoop to steal
If your treasures are high enough.

✽ ✽ ✽ ✽

They asked me if I took a nap
I said no truthfully
I could not say I took a nap
When it had taken *me*.

✽ ✽ ✽ ✽

When I am gone
Just let them say
That every hour of every day
He lived for sixty minutes.

Chicago

The nurse from Kankakee
Has a personality
Like a big red apple
Peeping, half-concealed
From out her verdant Shangri-la
Wearing a smile
That makes the heart beat quicker.
To glimpse her is to stop and stare
—And know desire to pick her.

Friend in the Philippines

The smile she wears is not for sale
It's free for all to share
Like sunshine on a shady trail
It makes a bright spot there.

Quiet and a wee bit shy
Her personality is sweet
Any wonder then that I
Her friendship deem a priceless treat?

No Favorite Flavor

In Manila
Where the women
Are more chocolate
Than vanilla
Here's a bit of knowledge I acquired.
Although blondes
They may prefer
Gentlemen will not demure
Accepting any substitute
—Femininity the only trait required.

Manilha

He spelled Manilha with an aitch
And I, from curiosity
Asked him why he put an aitch
Where it should never be.

"Of course, I put an aitch in there
And I think it no disgrace
There should be an aitch in it somewhere
'Cause it's such an aitch of a place."

Sunrise-Sunset*

'Twas in Luzon I realized
Two truths I'm not forgetting
No magic is there like the sunrise
—No splendor like its setting.

*In appreciation of Pacific sunsets—from old Fort Santiago looking westward toward Bataan

Overseas Time

I went ten thousand miles away
And stayed ten thousand years
I overcame ten thousand woes
With their corresponding fears.

But when at last I homeward sped
The joy of sweet returning
Was recompense for all the time
The heartache and the yearning

Ten thousand years at last elapsed
As time's swift charger spurred he
I went a boy of twenty-eight
Returned—a man of thirty.

USAT *Admiral Hughes*

As she gently rides at anchor
A sight she is to see
Beauty in her every line
Her size and symmetry.

She's not a super-luxury ship
With glistening brass and chrome
And yet with me she's strictly tops
—She's going to take me *home*.

Golden Gate

O Golden Gate, I couldn't wait
To keep our date in forty-eight
I had to come, I couldn't stay
Your call was clear, though far away
And now I'm here I have no kicks
With Christmas near in forty-six.

Troop Train

Onward through the day and night
She plunges with a might
Born of steam and steel and coal
Snarling from her very soul
Defiance—then stops to let a freight go by
Not heeding the impatient cry and curse
Of men, who think there's nothing worse
Than delay en route to be discharged
—Then hurtles on.

Part III

The Ladies

A few of the many I have known, including my three sisters, Esther, Susie (Sue), and Alice. I finally succumbed to an urge to write a verse about my mother, even knowing my tribute would be inadequate.

An International Beauty

This lady of mixed ancestry
Of countenance is fair
She has Germanic features
And flaxen Nordic hair;
Her eyes and breasts are Irish
She has charm and grace to spare
She's blest with legs from Paris
—With a London derriere.

Esther

To have known a Lady Esther
Is a dream not all achieve
Esther's an experience
Almost too much to believe.
Superwoman, before they came to be;
A doctor, teacher, musician
Designer, artist, seamstress, she
Has talents more than can be named.
She's horticulturist and cook
And if she so desired
She could write a book.
With a capacity to bear, to do
To love and be forgiving
With eagerness and joy
A lifelong zest for living.
Suffice it just to say—
"To have known our Esther
Is to turn our Esther-days
Into lovely memories."

Sue

How do we remember Sue?
Like a flower-freckled meadow
Under skies of sheerest blue
Her song was melody;
Her music and her life had style
What music couldn't do for her
Was accomplished by her smile.
Her smile, her music, and her way
Would brush away the darkest clouds
And bring to us a sunny day.
Ah yes! we remember Sue . . .

Alice

Alice is my *little* sister
Her presence a comfort to all
So easy and uncomplicated
So very vulnerably small.
Her face and her life
The calmness and the sudden smile
Reflect an elegant simplicity.
She is simply honest, simply sincere
With a majestic serenity.
Simply loving, deserving of love
Simply "dear little sister" to me.

Mom

An error of omission?
No poem for my mother
—Perhaps, but then
Considering how many other
Angels have escaped my pen
She's in the best of company
And needs no paltry rhyme from me.

How can I do poetic justice
With my poor pathetic verse?
How properly enshine a mother
Who was teacher, doctor, nurse
Farmer, gardener, cook, and baker?
She did what needed to be done
A loving mother, friend, homemaker
—A dozen women all in one.

Let her wear her halo lightly
Having done with tasks on earth
Angelic chores now suit her rightly
—Angel was She from her birth.

Inez

Renown, popularity, worldwide acclaim
And elusive, evasive, unpredictable fame
Leave me, in wonder, to ponder this wrong—
How come "Amazing Grace" has a song
To make her remembered the whole year long
While "Incredible Inez," charms all but unknown
Is immortalized only in my heart and home?

Hurry Back Anyway, Hon

Absence makes the heart grow fonder?
I don't see how that could be
When I love you all that I can love
While you're right here with me.

Gift List—for Inez

All the love that I have (husbandly type)
All kinds of services both day and night
Along with the chores that I'll cheerfully do
I'll always remember to say "I love you"
And appreciate all that she means in my life
My lovely, my lovee, my lover, my wife.

PS: Comic Sequel

For the one that I'm kissin'
An ear that will listen
Is a need that she has, I find
And if that's not enough
When the going gets tough
I will give her a piece of my mind.

Mandy

Whenever we wish for a little girl
We wish for a girl like Mandy
One that's pretty and pert, charming and smart
And sweet as ribbon candy

But since that wish will never come true
We'll replace that hope with another
—That as Mandy grows up, she'll grow up to be
A lady a lot like her mother.

Daughter-in-Law

The lovely, fragile, blessed bride
Is radiant as she stands beside
Her husband, he the thoughtful boy
So suddenly turned man.
To her all happiness and joy
For bringing to this sonful clan
Those special gifts we're mindful of
And most of all—her special love.

Carol I

O Carol, of the winsome smile
With laughter like a sparkling stream
At what moment past a little while
Did you tiptoe as in a dream
Into our hearts?
Then as we gently locked the door
There you'll remain forevermore.

Carol II

We simply wanted you to know
"Best wishes" follow where you go
And when more accolades are due
We'll be there with much love for you.

Love the yuletide season
With its music, gifts, and fun
Love the lovely Carols
—Especially the *one.*

Mary, Dental Hygenist par Excellence

A working girl's not hard to find
Less likely to spy the other kind
But in this world of women's lib
Of all who came from Adam's rib
We've something special in Mary.

She does her job especially well
If we confide, she doesn't tell
Her cheery chatter all the while
Amuses us; her winning style
Just makes us want to tarry.

We always hope that she'll be there
To serve with special dental care
And when the job she does is done
I'd match our smile with anyone
—My first smile is for Mary.

Appreciation

Ladies have so many ways
Of making themselves dear
Some are good to look at
Some are nice to hear
Some come with inspiration
Some bring ecstasy—but
Who brings the birthday brownies
Makes Brownie points with me.

Welcome, Meara Ann
(To a son's adopted daughter.)

We've long had instant pudding
Instant coffee's here to stay
There are instant oats for breakfast
"Instant winner" games to play.

These "instants" of convenience
Are supposed to set us free
From portions of our daily tasks
And domestic drudgery.

They don't excite us greatly
These we can take or leave
A really special advent
It takes to make us believe.

And hearts of ours are set aglow
That by the grace of God above
In her time of need, a little child
Found instant family, instant love.

Elaine

Mirror, mirror on the wall
Who's the fairest of them all?

"All the others pale and wane
Fairest ever's sweet Elaine."
Her charm and grace, as fresh as dew
Her winsome smile—they'll win you, too.

Melissa

To know her means
Memories ever after.
Her sunny smile
Sweet lilting laughter
Her songbird voice
Will never let
Us, who have seen and heard
—Forget.

Sew What? Sue

So you've decided you will sow.
Sew what, say I, you were never so-so
You've always been
So talented, so sunny sweet
So nice a niece, so superneat
So extra special, so Bo-Peep
So makes one want to be a sheep
So whatsoever you may sow
—Sew may you reap.

Queen Susan

Must be you've never met her
If you don't know who I mean
When I extol the praises of
Susan, the Queen of the Scene.
What scene? you say, no matter
Could be any scene at all
Choir practice or a party
Or a fancy costume ball.
When at work or even home
In fact, just anywhere
Susan's the Queen of the Scene
Anytime she's *there*! ! !

Sweet Sue

Sing of girls of wealth or style
Or of the girls with beauty blest
But Susan, of the quick, sweet smile
Will always outcharm all the rest.

Life may dreary, dull, or sad be
Till her presence, cheery, bright
Brings us joy and makes us glad we
Know her laughter, happy, light.

Years fly as loved ones soon depart
But time nor tears can e'er erase
From the albums of our hearts
Susan's sweet and smiling face.

Glenda

They say that bunnies bring the eggs
We find on Easter morn
I think that kind of thinking
Is just a can of corn
'Cause Easter eggs are always laid
By big birds in the sky
—Bunnies are too busy
Baking chocolate birthday pie!!

Fiction, Fun, and Fantasy, Together with Some Poetry

I've heard some army sergeants
And their words would burn your ears.
I've heard lumberjacks and truckers and the like,
And cowboys talking tough to uneducated steers
Use language that is beautiful to Tom and Pat and Mike.
A mechanic barks a knuckle, can't print those words, you know
A hammer hits a thumb, the cussin's fouler than the blow.

But for sheer linguistic splendor
There is no close contender
To a lady, name of Glenda
When she caught her body, tender
In the blender—and she let her feelings show.

October Fantasy

Now listen, Cinderella
You know I'm the kind of fella
That would furnish you a chariot if I could
But my pumpkin crop is naught
And all the mice I've caught
For chariot-pulling uses are no good.
But let's dream a little, Cindy
And pretend (instead of windy)
I'm Prince Charming with the slippers made of glass;
Until midnight tolls the hour
You're a princess in full flower
So enjoy it—while the happy hours pass.

Mary

A lady I know
(Who she is I won't say)
Personifies flaws in proposed ERA.
She demands equal treatment
And isn't impressed
That I already hold her
ABOVE all the rest.

Agnes, Citizen of the Year

She never needs to be told
Someone is hungry, needy, cold
That folks take comfort just to know
Someone cares, at times when morale is low.

An instinct tells her unerringly
To help and to serve unsparingly
Whether it be food or just a ride
Whatever the need, it is supplied.

For gifts of baked goods she is known
And for the compassion she has shown
To any and all who could use a hand.
She is ever willing to take a stand

For community, church, and neighborhood.
Her only vocation is doing good
All that she does is with a smile
—As she cheerfully goes that second mile.

Elma

Whatever role she is asked to play
She always gives her best
Mother, teacher, leader, friend
When called she meets each test.
Sweet music wafts upon the air
Where otherwise is none
Ask her for accompaniment
And it's as good as done.
She makes the world a better place;
Her gentle smile and modest grace
Are shared by all she knows or meets.
A happy heart and willing hands
She lends to many civic feats.
So if planning a popular project
Or plotting a tenuous trend
Seek Elma, she'll be there to help you
A friend of all—to all, a *friend*.

Saint Patrick's Day

A colleen born with Irish eyes
With attributes that make love rise
Should on this day of wearin' green
Be treated like an Irish queen.
Don't fret it that the shamrock's small
(We can't see leprechauns at all)
And little things large love convey
To steal an Irish heart away.

Erin Go Bragh

So a shamrock it was you were wanting?
Well, by golly, begorra, my friend
I wanted to send you a shamrock
But things didn't work out as I planned.
Still, I won't send a shillelagh
Or give you the back of me hand
'Cause I want to know that I raillegh
Think the Protestant Irish are GRAND!

I'm a Regular United Nations, but—This Is Saint Patrick's Day

There's a little bit o' English in me
And I guess a little bit o' German, too.
My friends insist that Scotch is in me person
And some might say I'm somethin' of a Jew.

It's true that I'm more lovin' that a Frenchman
And I always am a Russian fro and to
But it's shore I had the luck o' the Irish
—To have known a girl like you.

Irish Lass

We know that there's no harm in
Tellin' you how charmin'
An Irish lass is, any time of year
But let no one try to bar me
From the spreadin' of the blarney
Now that Old Saint Patrick's Day is here.

So with lilting Irish song
And a rhyme to help along
We'll do our best to tell you how we feel
Irish lass, oh how we love you
May the Irish saints above
Keep you sound and safe and sweet
—And ours for real.

Lovely Lady from Down Under

A lovely young lady from Perth
Was delightful in height and in girth
Her memorable style
Was matched by her smile
And a charm of considerable worth.

The Saga of the Sage and the Sagittarians

> *Sagittarians can be supersensitive; these natives are intent on preserving their integrity. They often remarry former spouses. They seldom ask favors, preferring to perform services. These are the travelers, the erudite individuals who can brightly express their feelings. Sagittarians are no angels, but there is an appealing gentleness to them that can be seductive.*
> —From a January 3, 1973, horoscope.

"No angels are they" the sage opines
But what does he know of heavenly signs?
And what of angels? An expert is he?
Has he ever known one—or two—or three?
This self-styled prophet is a phony, I say
A pencil pusher who writes for pay
And anyone knows that should only be done
For pleasure, for friends, or for legible fun.
So I suggest this out-and-out fraud
Can't distinguish an angel from a bawdy broad
While the Sagittarians I could name
Would cause many another angel shame.
And the angelic things they constantly do
Are unhampered by wings or by halos askew
But they act the role of human so well
That no one will know—unless I tell.
So soothsayer, know ye where ye may go—
Leave our angels to *us* in the heavenly know.

Part IV
Love

A favorite topic due to having given and received so much.

Love Is New

The poems have all been written
All of the songs have been sung
Everything's been invented
All of the bells have been rung.

All of history has happened
Nothing's new under the sun
'Cause the newest of things is the oldest
All that was started is done.

Original sin has long been a myth
New virture nowhere to be found
New ideas have only been pilfered
From those that have long been around.

But this wonderful love for a woman
Is something *incredibly new*
Never was true love so wondrous and deep
—Darling, until I loved you.

Let's Face It—It's Bigger than Both of Us
or
We're Young and Can Afford to Wait
or
Let's Wait for Something More Permanent on a Trial Basis

Forget about that quickie deal
I'm sure you must know how I feel.

Though I may do the "playboy" bit
From flower to flower as I flit

My thoughts forevermore are true
With dreams and *memories* of *you*

The torch still flames and ne'er abates
"All things will come to he who waits."

Love Impossible

Unlikely, unexpected, unsolicited
From beginnings oh! so small
As like a tiny seed
Though lodged in barren rock
Still finds the nourishment
The warmth and all its needs
And then as if the utterly impossible to mock
It seems to thrive and grow
And by its very power to enthrall
The two of us—we know
Our love is not impossible at all.

Valentine

Some folks think I'm pretty cool
The "thinking" type, nobody's fool
But little know they what I hide—
The passion and the flame inside
The secret thoughts and daring dreams
Go flowing by like silvery streams
That self-destruct my pensive mood
—I think of you and come unglued.

Thank You

Thank you for your tender look and gentle sweet caress
Thank you for the things you do that mean my happiness
Thank you for the way you show how much you really care
And for the way you let me know when needed you'll be there.
Thanks for tolerating the intolerable the very best you can
Thanks for making me believe that I'm *some* kind of man
And thanks for all the lovely things you always say and do
But most of all thanks for your love and thanks for being *you*.

Happy Birthday

Now you know I wouldn't rib you
But instead of Eve, I find
A spritely Sagittarian drifts dreamily through my mind
And a still, small voice is speaking
It urges me to say—
Happy, happy, happy birthday
Just because I feel that way.

Heart Felt

To the one I love so much
With the skin I love to touch
I thought of giving you my heart
Then realized the fact
I gave it to you years ago
—You never gave it back.

And so I hope it's still around
Receiving loving care
'Cause it's the only one I had
—I never had a spare.

Love Me Now

Happiness, elusive, fleeting
Never waits on our commands
While our throbbing hearts are beating
Let us grasp it in our hands

Wrest from life the joy of living
All tomorrows disavow
Give our love and in the giving
Gain the sweet, bright here and now.

For the past is gone forever
And the future is in doubt
Love me now—and may we never
Let the flame of love go out.

We Love Her

Not so much for what she does
Nor yet for the way she does it
But for the person that she *is* . . .

Not so much for what she says
As for her way of saying it
As she "tells it like it is" . . .

For her way of caring, loving, sharing
Never ever sparing of herself . . .
Her human-ness shines through
Along with gentle faith, ne'er overpowering.
Of the many, many "why we love hers"
—These are just a few.

Pagan Mug Song

I just want to see myself
Close to you on the kitchen shelf
Handle to handle and butt to butt
No one knows what goes on
When the door is shut.

Nobody will peek
And no word will we speak,
Never know when a place may be bugged
Though the saucers may guess—we'll never confess
Baby, you're gonna know you've been mugged.

November Nocturne

I might forget the first time we met
And erase all the times we've been blue
But I'll always remember a night in November
Of me, and the moonlight, with you.

No sound of a bird or a tree toad was heard
In silence, stars peered from above
The better to see; there were only we three
You and me in the moonlight—with love.

Neither the trees nor the soft sighing breeze
Will tell of the passion we knew
The moonlight's soft beams mingled memories and dreams
Of love in the moonlight with you.

An All-Holiday Wish

For Saint Patrick's or Easter's or April Fool's
I love you so much, I just can't play it cool
May you have everything that you love is my plea
Up to, and especially, including me.

Pinned

You said that you would like a pin
To wear for all to see—
This pin is old, experienced
Reliable, like me.
As for size, 'tis obvious
It simply dwarfs them all
Just the way my love for you
Makes other loves seem small.

Jumper

Here it's leap year once again, but
How can I think of leaping when
That's not my heart that you hear thumping
It's my feet—you keep *me jumping*
Hoping you'll be satisfied.
My epitaph will read, "He Tried"—
Tried to give you happiness
And sweet contentment.
May God bless.

Young Love

We've loved in lonely meadows on some sunny afternoons
Beneath the moon and under starlit skies
The memories linger on of when we've danced to many tunes
Those memories are not made of stuff that dies
Though some of the rest pass the memory test
One night I remember the best—
You were a charge of dynamite and I such a short, short fuse
When we bared our butts in the buttercups
And all sweet love broke loose.

Valentine II

I suppose, perhaps, you noticed
That I didn't make a fuss
When Valentine's Day came around
It wasn't much to us;
We don't need a *special* day
To be a Valentine
'Cause every day, come what may
My love is yours—and yours is mine

Disappointed

You didn't come and even though
You only said you might
My optimistic straw-clutching mind
Interpreted this to mean that you would
Keep our rendezvous, and so
The disappointment was as keen
As if a promise almost had been
Broken.

Love Changes

I'll never ever be the same
My life has changed and since you came
There's hope where there had been despair
There's love and knowing that you care
And I will never be the same.

When you're away, it's different, too
'Cause dreams and memories of you
Come all unbidden to my mind;
My eyes may close but still I find
Your face, your smile come drifting through.

Our world will never be the same
Our song's a gentle, sweet refrain
That floats from earth to Heaven above;
Because we plumbed the depths of love
—Our world will never be the same.

Birthday = ?

The lady has a birthday—in fact, she's had a few
I don't know just how many, but I'm sure of twenty-two;
"Too young," you say, "December-May," that very well could be
So I'll just wait till next year—*then* she'll be *twenty-three!*

Good-Luck Charm

I'm selfish and so, wherever you go
This good-luck charm I want you to wear
Just keep it about you, 'cause I can't do without you
There's no telling you how much I care;
Whatever you do, may God watch over you
And protect, guide, and bless from above
Though you may be afar, wherever you are
You *can't* leave our circle of love.

Loved One

The sun gets up in the morning
Just to bask in the warmth of your smile
And the dew that falls without warning
Tries to match your soft caress
Your gentleness.

Raindrops in the soft spring showers
Do their best to imitate your style
As sweetly they kiss bright spring flowers;
They bring happiness
And everyone bless.

Of your fresh sweetness
The blossoms borrow;
Hope of love's completeness
Is the promise of tomorrow.

The sun, the moon, and the stars above
Flowers and breezes and clouds all yearn
To be with you in your special love
Under the bright blue sky
—And so do I.

All My Love

Like water from a deep, clear well
Comes love—for reasons none can tell.
How much love can one man give?
Just all he has, while he shall live.

Togetherness

There is no happiness unless you're happy
Uncaring is the world—unless you care
Loneliness is all when we're apart
The pain and joy, each other's not to share.
Forever is the time we're not together
An hour's but a moment when you're there
There is no love without your love
No hope—except the hope that lovers dare.

Love Poem

How can you ever know how much I miss you?
How can you realize how much I care?
What rules can determine the snowiness of the snow?
How measure the power of unselfish prayer?

When you're not in my arms how empty the feeling
The while my heart is full of love for you.
How can you know the yearning, the flames of a love that's
    burning
—Unless you feel that way too.

Love Poem II

When you're away the world is dark
And skies are gray, what was a lark
No pleasure brings what was our song
No longer swings, and hours are long.

But when you're near the darkness goes
You're all that's dear, your sweet smile shows
You know I care, and should you call
I'll surely be there—and love is all.

More Love Poems

I know that it's been a long, long time
Since I've regaled you with song or with rhyme
But nothing has changed, nothing has gone
It's just that—those *old* songs keep lingering on
Reminding us both of a love that is true
Old love and old love songs are *better* than new
So play an old love song I wrote yesterday
And know that my love for you grows every day.

This I know—I love you so
And want you close, so soft and warm
To sleep wrapped in your loving arms
And wake to find you smiling there
With fingers running through my hair
While all my loving thoughts of you
Go running wild, love's ever new.
I love you. Ah! I truly do.

Ever Together

Inevitably, a friend will ask—
"Your wife is touring Europe
While you're home here cutting grass?
That arrangement's mighty strange.
Has your mutual affection
Undergone a subtle change?
Do you worry not at all
That the time lapse and the distance
May, between you, build a wall?"

"Quite the opposite, my friend.
For every lonely hour apart
Many, many more we'll spend
Appreciating, each, the other
And as we love
Won't let love smother
Individual wants and needs;
We'll both have fruit
Not stems and seeds.
In short, it's love in every way.
I love enough to let her go—
She loves enough to let me stay."

Hurry Back Again

"Out of sight is out of mind"
Folks always said that this was true
And yet while you're away
I seem to think of ought but you
You're in my thoughts and in my heart
A thousand times I see your face
It matters not that we're apart
My arms recall your sweet embrace
In short—no more the truth I ponder
It's "absence makes the heart grow fonder."

Alone

Lonely was tonight
Though it was Saturday;
The crowd was laughing, friendly, bright
At least for most it seemed that way.
Would you believe I was alone
Suspended there in time and space?
This night that should have been our own
Is gone; it never left a trace
—You weren't there.

It's Saturday and I prayed again
For you, for us, for love's sweet sake;
He didn't answer, not right then
Perhaps, next time He'll be awake.

Lonely

My heart is on vacation
Whenever you're away
That's the way it's going to be
Until you're home to stay.

Things I should do are left undone
I'm dreaming all the while
Of you, your eyes, your arms, your lips
And longing for your smile.

But when you're near, sweet music
Fills the air and bells do chime
Birds sing, joy is everywhere
—My heart is working OVERTIME.

December 16 Birthday

A birthday looms large on the scene
A day for my wife to be queen.
Though she's been thirty-nine
Time after time—
She'll *always* be "sweet sixteen."

In Defense of Separate Vacations

Although there's an ocean between us
Really we're never apart
No mountain or ocean divides us
You're close in my mind and my heart.

Better temporarily lonely
With love growing stronger each day
Than constantly side by side to be
While love's going farther away.

Though apart, yet ever together
That's the way for you and for me
While others so seemingly close
Are *apart,* as a couple can be.

Think Happy

The happiness I bring to you
Is all the happiness I need;
You're why I do the things I do
I write and hope that you will read.
Thoughts of you are what I think
I listen, hoping you to hear;
It's up to you if I swim or sink
When far away I want you near.

All the assurances that I need
Is just in knowing that you care
That you'll be beside me where I lead;
All love is in the love we share.

Misnomer

Why do they call them "the golden years"
Those few that are left in the autumn of life?
Is there really nothing more precious than gold
Or will those years be that hard and cold?
Let's pray that ours will be soft as whipped cream
And warm as a kitten, stretched out by a fire
Tender as buds just beginning to flower
With love that outweathers the wind and the shower.
With moments of love, relaxed and content
We'll rejoice as life's beautiful autumn nears;
Each day together, a heavenly gift
—Let others suffer the "golden years."

Independence Day

It's the Fourth of July—just another day
'Cause the one I love is far away;
Nothing festive, nothing bright
Can cheer me, either day or night.
The Independence (I don't need)
Accents the lonely life I lead
And Declarations, old or new
With no one to declare them to
Make me eager for days we'll spend
When on each other we'll depend

Though love of country, deeply etched
Within my heart still burns—
There won't be any fireworks
Until *my wife* returns.

Longing

In stillness I seek
And in silence do find
There's no need to speak
You're there in my mind.
Your tender caresses
Are memories of when
I knew love that blesses
—And long to again.

Lonely II

Suffer? Yes, of course I do!
Those desolate hours I'm not with you
Go dragging into endless days
Of sullen, gloomy blues and grays
And no one knows the poignant pain
The loneliness that strikes again
To warn us not to be apart—
It's in my head, and in my heart.

Together Forever

As the world goes 'round
And time wings past
May our love be timeless
Well built to last.
When lyrics on our deaf ears fall
Our "Together" songs may we recall.
So let fly the years, wherever they go
Our love will be music
The tempo—sweet and slow.

Signs of Spring

When drab old winter slips away
And skies are blue instead of gray
Thoughts of you like birds a-wing
Keep coming back, and with the spring
You know where young man's fancy turns.
As long deprived, the heart then yearns
For pleasures of a bygone year
Companionship that I hold dear.

I hope your love for me is true
After all, it's your spring, too.
Let's find a nook, a sunny spot
With violet and forget-me-not.
We'll fan the blaze and stir the fire
Evoke the passions of desire
And love will bloom in vernal glade
That dormant throughout winter laid.

It Happens

That every once in a lifetime
There is someone like you
And every once is a lifetime
I find I must say and do
The every-once-in-a-lifetime things
That reveal how much I love you.
And with all my heart, I'm hoping
That deep in *your* heart there'll be
An every-once-in-a-lifetime love
That happens to you, for me.

I Care

I know—
How quiet it is in the house
When nobody is rattling the pans
How lonely when nobody
Is expected home soon
How cool when nobody
Is warm in the room
How empty the bed
When nobody's to share
How solitary, with no one to hear
"I love you, appreciate you, and I care."

Longing and Waiting

"It must be kind of lonesome
With your wife away so long."
That's what I hear, but I reply,
"It's not so bad, my love is strong
I keep quite busy through the day.
At night I write or watch tv
I sleep well and I eat OK"
And, of course, I have your memory.
—But yes, it's lonely, I confess
You're everything I lack, but
It would be so much lonelier
If I didn't know you'd be back.

I'll Love You More

Some folks think love is just for kids
But we know that's not true;
Those kids don't know enough to know
The things that love can do.
They haven't lived or loved enough
Their love is much too new
And I'll love *you* more at eighty-four
Than I did at twenty-two.

Some folks think dreams are just for kids.
It's not that way at all
Dreams are for all of the seasons
Winter, spring, summer, and fall.
Those kids don't have Experience
Experience, with a capital E
And I'll love you more at eighty-four
Than I did at fifty-three.

Yes, love and dreams *are* just for kids
For kids like you and me;
Dreaming and loving are portions of life
The way life ought to be.
Dreaming and loving, caring and sharing
Add up to being alive
And I'll love you more at eighty-four
Than I did at sixty-five

I'll love you more at eighty-four
Than I ever did before.

Honey, I Love You Enough

To go with you 'times I'd rather not
To cool it when I'd like it hot
To be there when you'd like to play
To try to stay out of your way
When you're not in a friendly mood.
I try to be a well-dressed dude
When handsome escort is your need
Adjust my moves to match your speed.
When you're at work, I never phone
You're busy, so I wait alone
And I care enough to let you go
Without me—I know you know
I'll be right here, watching, waiting
With my heart anticipating
On your return from foreign clime
With love, bounded not by space or time.

Short Sweet Memories

We both know that life
Has its ups and downs;
We've listened to Loves' Old Sweet Song
And our memories will be
Sweeter, for you and for me
'Cause we won't have to remember so long.

(Or so long to remember.)

Sixty-five Approacheth

Some folks may say I'm "over the hill"
But if they don't, *I* never will.
At sixty-five life's more serene
An interesting, even exciting scene.
More time to hear, more time to see
Sounds and sights that eluded me
In years I spent, without remorse
As an active member of the labor force.

Each day's adventure is a treat
Each night's repose especially sweet
And I offer thanks to God above
That I'm sixty-five—
And still in love.

Remembering

I can't help remembering
Your tender smile, the subtle way you cling
The warmth and softness of your lips
The way my heartbeat always skips
When I see the joy and laughter in your face
And know your gentle arms when we embrace
Your sweet voice murmuring, "Right," when you agree
Your eyes as they light up with ecstasy
The joy that only your caress can bring
—Our love won't let me stop remembering.

I'd Love to Share

I'd love to share the bird calls heard at dawning
Your gentle smile touched by first rays of the sun
Intimate visits over coffee in the morning,
The plans, the dreams, the work, the play, the fun.

I'd love to share the view from highest places
Races 'cross the meadows, the hikes on wooded hills
The setting sun, the sky's wide-open spaces
The triumphs, all the heartaches, and the thrills.

I'd love to share sweet memories in the making
The waking of your tender love and care;

I'd love to share a life of love and laughter
Along with tears, as sorrows we'd go through
It's you I'll love from now till ever after;
I'd love to share—everything with you.

Mind Full of You

They say that love comes from the heart
That once one's pierced by Cupid's dart
One nevermore will be the same
And in the heart will burn loves' flame;

But I think love is in the mind
And that is why I always find
That thoughts and dreams come shining through
Along with memories of you.

Between the Lines

This afternoon the mailman brought your letter
And for me once more the bright sun shines;
There's nothing that could make me feel much better
When I read about your love—between the lines.

My heart skipped as I opened up your note
Love was there, the symptoms and the signs
That love was mine, I knew, by what you never wrote
And I read about it—right between the lines

Oh, how I miss you, and how I wish you
Would ever be near;
You're my everything, and to me you bring
All that I hold dear.

My answer to you is now on the way
Although you're not the type that sighs and pines
Still, I hope you'll read the things I didn't say
—The love that's written in between the lines.

Lobelia and Me

We don't make lots of noise
Or holler "Olé"
We don't shout like the big flowers do
Our sweet little smile
Just whispers to say
When you are not here
WE ARE BLUE.

Homebody

Don't care for ritzy nightclubs
Or swinging all-night bars
That goes for fancy furniture
And late-model luxury cars.
Don't get me stylish new clothes
My old ones do just fine
Don't drag me to the theater
Or even out to dine.
I don't want reservations
To fly the friendly skies
Around the world or coast to coast
That's for those other guys.
I never wanted anything
In all the world, it's true
'Cept staying home and loving
—Being loved by you.

Eyeful Power

Cupid did it with his arrow
Just as God's eye's on the sparrow
Girl, I've got my eye on you;
Tell you what I'm going to do.
I'll love you till you holler "Ouch"
And I will be an awful grouch
Until I hear you say that *you*
Are going to love *me* that way, too.

A Christmas Love

I love you with a Christmas love
More wondrous love there could not be.
Then came as if from heaven above
The light of logic revealed to me
This happy truth—

As loving waves embrace the shore
I love you so much all the year
I couldn't love you more;
It's just that Christmastime is here
—And so is love.

Christmas Loving

In the crush of Christmas shopping
In the rush for Christmas cheer
Let's remember yuletime's greatest gift
Is LOVE through all the year.

The way we treat each other
The way we daily live
All the love I have is yours
Because—you have so much to give.

Élan

I waken in the early morning
When the day is just a-borning.
The grass is wet with nocturne's dew
The sky is not yet thinking "blue."
The birds begin their morning cry
As through the fresh moist air they fly
And breezes cause the leaves to blur
As sighing scarely do they stir.
The sweet soft essence of the dawn
Arouses life as life goes on.
Then I reflect on the eager way
I start with joy each bright new day.
So love God's gifts the way I do
'Cause all *my* love I give to you

Anniversary

You asked what *anniversary* meant—
It means another year has *went.*
It's gone forever and in its stead
A few less hairs upon my head.
But twelve whole months of life and love
Are like a gift from Heaven above.
And there are memories we hold dear
—We're happy that we had the year.

PS: Yes, it's anniversary "three"
Not much in terms of eternity
But, in fairness, let's give the devil his due
—It's certainly more than one or two.

It Happens Every Time

It happens every time
Whenever we're apart
That lonesome feeling that comes stealing
Deep into my heart.

It happens every time
As soon as you're not there
Remembering you will leave me blue
Reminding me how very much I care.

So here am I alone again
The lonely blues are knockin' on my door
As sure as there are stars above
I'll hoard my kisses, save my love
Till I hold you in my arms once more.

It happens every time—

Blossoms All

Roses remind me of you
I wish that I could send some
Yet nothing does what black-eyed Susans do;
In simple humbleness they then come
Inviting your attention and trying for your smile.
Because of you, sweet peas are sweet
Forget-me-nots beseech you all the while
And only bloom in hopes that they will meet
You, to memorize your laughter
The loveliness and beauty in your face;
Then pray that they'll remember ever after.

Baby, I'll Be There

There's an energy crisis and gasoline prices
Just went up again today;
Farther on down the line, the No Gasoline sign
Put my car out of business to stay.

So I left it to rust, made a Nashville or Bust
Sign, in hopes I could hitch a ride.
I give it a try, but the drivers speed by
And I'm left with what's left of my pride.

Somehow I've gotta get down this road
I can't reap wild oats that I've never sowed.

My thoughts are of when you said, "Come back again"
And offered your sweet love to share;
I know I will pay, I may walk all the way
But, Baby, I'll be there—
You can bet that I'll be there.

Uninvolved

"Let's not get too involved," said she.
A half a year has passed since we
Have either spoken and/or met.
How uninvolved can we get?
As for me, no pangs of guilt—
My heart's involved right to the hilt.

Bound to Be Free

I was free as the breeze, I could do as I please
No one else was arranging *my* life;
My problems were solved, just not getting involved
With a sweetheart, a family, or wife.

On life's stormy sea, I was captain and crew
Didn't need a co-captain or mate;
I'd found my own style, behind a permanent smile
I was completely in charge of my fate.

I tried to forget every new face I met
Life was simple and neat as a pin
But I started to doubt, I felt like an "out"
While everyone else was an "in."

Then I met *you*, and the truth busted through
With remarkable hindsight, I see
In the depths of all souls, there are dual controls
—Only the lonely are free.

Mother's Day (Out)

I'm glad you're not my mother
Wouldn't want her to be you
'Cause mothers try to make one
Do the things they want you to.

They try to change a man around
To change his style of life
Don't be a mother to me
Just be a lover, friend, and wife.

Part V

Grandchildren

These several verses were written either about grandchildren or to amuse them. Grandchildren I would highly recommend to anyone. There were only three when "Granddad" was written; there are nine now and the first is a college graduate. Time and grandchildren wait for no man!

Grandchildren

How wondrous
Oh, how wonderful
Among things God has planned
It is that He made grandchildren
So absolutely GRAND!

Thoughts on Growing Up

A polliwog is not a frog
And yet someday it may be
The frog is *in* that polliwog
And you're a *man* to be.

Grandad

First to come along was Bill
And he was king and reigned until
Debbie Ann came on the scene
Then he shared the throne
With this preschool queen
Jonathan arrived of late
And he was surely worth the wait.

Though someone else's progeny
Each one of these belongs to me
It's great to hold them on my lap
We have no generation gap
There's true zest for living
Joy to be had
Just spoiling and loving them
—Being Grandad.

Vocation?

Oh, the "Goon in the Glen"
Has a place in the park
Where he dwells in a dismal den
He keeps a crude crock
And it's there after dark
That he crushes the rock
For the rock n' roll bands;
There he makes and mangles
The music and lyrics
—So nobody understands.

Moist and Misty

Why does the rain come down like spray
Or fog or dew instead of in drops?
It's really not a rainy day when
Moisture's no longer in plips and plops.

Unknown to us, mist comes to be
Perhaps, from small angels crying?
In the midst of the mist it's clear to me
—This mist is most mystifying.

Strange Bedfellow

He was always doing differently
The things that others did
Some said he was eccentric
Some called him "Crazy kid."
And then he started sleeping
The wrong way in his bed
With his head down at the bottom
And his feet up at the head
This went on for quite a while
Then gradually it showed
His feet woke up with headaches
His head was pigeon-toed.

April Foolishness

The fairy raised her magic wand
And whispered in my ear,
"Ask anything your heart desires
I'll do it for you, dear."

And so I asked the firstest thing
That popped into my head,
"Make me an Easter bunny
With long fuzzy ears," I said.
"Then I can lay the Easter eggs
And hide them all around
And little kids will laugh and shout
And make a joyful sound;
Meanwhile I'll scamper to and fro
And join in all the fun
A happy time will then be had
By each and every one."
The fairy sadly shook her head,
"I can't do that for you.
Ask something easier." she said,
"Within my realm to do."

So to the willing but unable fairy
Said I, "Then let's play it cool.
If I can't be the Easter Bunny
Can't I please be an April fool?
Not just this month but for the whole darn month.
Please do it for me, ma'am."

The fairy waved her magic wand
—And that is what I am!

Classroom Crisis

The kid came home from school today
And said, "Hey, Mom, oh, by the way
I've got a note from the teacher here.
It's wrinkled and crinkled, bad news, I fear."

The note read,
"Dear Parent,
An examination of head and hair
Revealed a lousy condition there;
Your child's infested with eggs and lice
A situation that's far from nice.
Exterminate promptly—that's the rule
Before that kid comes back to school."

Mom didn't panic or have a fit
She meditated for just a bit
Then vowed she'd give those lice a licking
Though the teacher, she felt, was just nitpicking.

Linguistically Speaking

I don't know Latin, Spanish, or Greek
English—the only language I speak
I can't translate in French or Chinese
In Tagalog or Turkish can't even say, "please."
Egyptian or Russian? Can't write a line
But body language?
I read and interpret just fine.

Broke It, Huh?

I've been involved with a cast in the past
And experience prompts me to say
It isn't much fun to be in a cast
Unless it's the cast of a play.

Lucky Break

A broken bone will surely mend
'Cause broken bones do heal
No one has ever perished
From a discomforting feel
So thank the Lord above you
For the charmed life you have led
And be grateful it was just your arm
'Stead of your pointy little head.

Here's a Mouthful

Now I brush my faithful teeth
Top and sides and underneath
Today they've bitten well, but then
Tomorrow they must bite again.

Eskimo Economics

Ukluk, the Eskimo, was a mighty hunter.
During the hunting season he killed several walruses and prepared the meat to use during the cold winter. The walrus fat he carefully packaged to take to the trading post to barter for supplies that he would need, that he could not make for himself or wrest from the frozen land in which he lived.

At the trading post, however, a serious disappointment awaited him as the trader said, "I'm sorry, Ukluk, but our storage is full of walrus fat. We won't be able to accept any more until the ship comes to transport that which we already have on hand. I'm sure we'll be able to handle it, if you can keep your walrus fat for six weeks."

This was a bad blow to the economy of Ukluk as he needed the supplies NOW, and his wail of protest filled the frozen North as he raised his eyes skyward and cried, "AM I MY BLUBBER'S KEEPER?"

Parapooch

This crazy teenage parakeet
Had always been a bit off beat
And though he never learned to speak
He listened, Baby, like a pro
And that is how he came to know
That eavesdropping can bring one pain
And so within his small bird brain
He got the word that we preferred
Instead of one small cagey bird
To have a dog instead.
At first it almost broke his heart
But then he vowed to do his part
To make us feel we had a pup;
So what he did was study up
On all the dog lore he could find
And yes, we thought that it was kind
Of strange when he began to yap and growl
And chew our shoes and bite the towel.
When he refused to eat his seed
Then knowing it was food he'd need
We got dog food (he'd learned to yip)
And gave him Gravy Train to sip.
He gave the mailman such a nip
He had to get a rabies shot
(We don't know if it took or not
'Cause frothing at the mouth a lot
Was what *he* always did);
The canine census taker came
And he flew off and hid.
He'd pant and slobber at the beak
And messed the rug six days a week
(He tried to do his very best)
But Sunday was his day of rest.

We got a collar and a leash
So we could walk him on the street;
He'd quite forgotten how to tweet
And so we thought, perhaps, that he
Would like a hydrant or a tree
But when his leg he tried to raise
He lost his balance—in a daze
He fell upon his furry head.
We thought that he was playing dead
But soon we found that life had fled
So now he's just a memory.
We buried him beneath the tree
And on the stone that marks his end
We wrote, "This bird-dog was our friend."

The moral in this catastrophe
Is "Be yourself"; don't try to be
What you are not
Or you'll end up
Being sad a lot.
The poor dumb bird was doomed to fail
—He never learned to wag his tail.

Fish Story

Let me tell you about a sad thing that happened at our house. When Alan left home, he left behind his aquarium of guppies and tropical fish, so we try to take care of them as best we can, feeding them each night at bedtime (mine, not the guppies). There is green vegetation taking over the bottom part of the tank, so if the water gets low, there is very little swim area for the occupants and they appear to be crowded. Last night I noted that the water level was down, so I added a gallon, which raised the water level about three inches.

Well, several of the younger guppies, inexperienced and lacking in judgment, suddenly found themselves in water over their heads. Still, they would have been okay if they had not panicked and forgotten the drown-proofing techniques and swimming skills taught them by their parents. Unfortunately, panic prevailed and the poor little teenaged guppies were doomed. We tried to revive them with mouth-to-mouth resuscitation but to no avail. The only decent thing left to do was to give them a naval burial (which means I buried their navels and consigned the rest of their bodies to a "watery grave"). "They would have wanted it that way."

Two of the youngsters were members of a rock group known as the "Guppies," and one composed choral arrangements for "Aquarius."

Moral

Little guppies, you should seek
The skills and knowledge of the wise.
Listen! when your parents speak;
They're smarter than you realize!!

Part VI

Battle of the Sexes

Some good-humored jibes at some of the differences between the sexes.

For Men Only

If there's one thing that worries a woman
It's something she ought not to know
But she'll manage to get at it somehow
If she has the least chance of a show.
Now, I'll wager ten cents to a million
This poem you've already read
'Cause I knew you'd get at it somehow
—If you had to stand on your head.

The Imperfect Man

I know I'm a disappointment
Not quite the kind of man
You had hoped would be the one
To fit exactly in your plan.

I don't feel a perfect failure
(Nobody's perfect) especially when
To be that kind of fella
Would take a dozen other men.

And I can't change completely
To become somebody new
But that same unswerving quality
Keeps my love strong and true.

Poor Shopper

Honey,
You know I love you
More than I can tell
And I'm in trouble once again
'Cause I don't shop that well
But you're a real good shopper
And there's hope for us yet
So be a good do-it-yourselfer
Then what you want
—Is what you get!

Filing Singly or Jointly?

Some men prefer their bachelorhood
Some like the married state;
This choice has been the topic
Of endless stern debate.
I've tried them both, in younger days
I enjoyed the single chase;
Then later on I played the role
Of a man in marital embrace.
There's no universal answer
Personal preference is the key;
I speak not for others, as for me
—Both were hard on my chastity.

When She Sends You Shopping

If she *sends* you at all
It's bound to be an experience
Go with caution, check that list
Before you go, some items may need
Clarification; that list may include
Anything from bird bibs to bunny undies.
Go with prevarication
Always bring the money home
Tell her the items were out of stock
Or the quality was too poor
Wrong size, or no place to park
Tell her anything as long as
You save your money.
She will show her appreciation
In the end—YOURS
And you are bound to get a kick out of it.

Composite Compulsive Cleaner

She must be the cleanest woman
The world has ever known
The thought of any speck of dust
Will turn her heart to stone.
She washes all the dishes
Even if they've not been used
And to find a latent fingerprint
Will not make her amused.
A sign upon her threshold
Will let you know the score,
"Wipe your feet on my welcome mat
Or don't come through my door."

The bedclothes all get laundered
When they're scarcely even soiled
Not just a rinse and dry job
They must be sudsed and boiled.
When you're finished in the bathroom
It had better look like new
The toilet and the washroom
And yes, the bathtub too.
She'd shoot you dead if you track in grass
She's got a forty-four
So wipe your feet on her welcome mat
Or don't come through her door.

Her windows all are spick and spanned
In truth they're just so shined
She has to keep the shades pulled down
To keep from going blind.
She's tidy when she makes a cake
(She kitchen's by the hour)
She always washes everything
The raisins, eggs, and cinnamon, the sugar and the flour.
You're lucky if she loves you
No one could love more
But wipe your feet on her welcome mat
Or don't come through her door.

When I come home at two A.M.
I try not to start a war
My shoes and socks are in my hand
And still she'll claim that my "dirty" feet
Left tracks upon the floor.
But my macho briefs get laundered
More than they ever did before
I wipe my feet on her welcome mat
And keep comin' through her door.
Better wipe *your* feet on her welcome mat
Or don't come through her door!

Cleanliness and Godliness?

(Sagittarius, November 22 to December 21: Remember the adage "Cleanliness is next to godliness" when it comes to those domestic tasks you're tempted to put off to another day.)

Strange bedfellows these.
Cleanliness to an extreme
Has been the rock that shattered
Matrimony's ship and love's sweet dream.
A house that's just too spic and span
Makes living hard for mortal man;
There's no way he can e'er compete
With keeping all so tidy, neat.
When every stain has been removed
Each speck of dust below, above
Each trace of lint from every room
There is no time or room for love.
And when he, disappointed, dies
Unfulfilled by love or lust
A fitting epitaph might be
"He loved alone—and bit the dust."

Rules of Rhyme

I early learned to write in rhyme
That "forever" is a long, long time
That always there will be a "moon"
To rhyme with words like "croon" and "June."

Now years have made me more mature
I love less often and more sure
The words that fit are like "forget"
It rhymes exactly with "regret."

So while romance needs must be served
Here's ample cause to come unnerved
—Poetic justice ruled that "cupid"
Will rhyme with nothing else but "stupid."

Wordy

My wife is a woman of very few words
Do you think that might make me elated?
No! she uses them over and over again
Till I wish that we weren't related.

Strike Three—Y'er Out!

Man is born, so I've been told
With two strikes on him; I prefer
To think that he has only one
Until the day that he meets *her*.

If she's in the groove, he may
Not get to first base, instead
He hits into a double play
Her tantalizing curves can knock him dead.

When he's single, he hopes to make a hit
And having made a mighty clout
He doubles, and from that time on
He simply can't get out.

The day he's showered with shoes and rice
He thinks he'll make a home run;
It's an error or a sacrifice
—His chances? Absolutely none.

She umpires and keeps the score
She makes the ground rules, too;
No use to argue or implore
Or, brother, you are through.

We just can't win, our fate is sealed
The moment that we fall
But, Honey, let's you take the field
—And you and I "play ball."
PS: Already I have been at bat
And hit my own "home run"
We just can't win, no doubt of that
—But losing is such fun.

Loser

A man and wife whose wedded life
Was something short of bliss
An argument were having
And I, an unintentional witness.

Hot and heavy raged the fray
A battle keen and vicious
'Cause women, running short of words
Resort to throwing dishes.

When the issue was decided
And the din had died away
No vitriolic language
Was there left for them to say.

I asked that sorry-looking man
If he rued the life he'd led;
His haggard face and haunted eyes
He raised to mine and said,

"It's not that I dislike dispute
Debate and I are friends
But just one time I'd like to be
The *winner*—when it ends."

By Choice

I *like* doing chores and errands
To satisfy wifely desires
It seems to me a privilege
To stoke those marital fires.

And a thing that I always appreciate
It makes my heart rejoice
Whenever she gives me tasks to do
She always give me a choice.

As for me, I try to choose wisely
And avoid love's tempestuous spells
I may never find out—*if I'm lucky*
What she might mean by *"or else."*

Feminine Mystique

God or Shakespeare once did say,
"The ways of women are wonderful and strange."
How else could one explain the way
A drop of dirty water in the sink or on the range
She can spot the moment she arrives
While a fresh bouquet of flowers
She can work around for hours
And never notice even that they're there;
And a brilliant sparkling toilet
That's so clean before we soil it
Doesn't rate a single comment or a stare.
But don't think that I'm complaining
Life is more than clouds and raining
And a woman is the sunshine of my life
Just remember there's a danger
That a woman may get stranger
Once she's said the vows that make of her—
A wife.

I Had This Dream

My wife, Burt Reynolds on her mind
Was rapt in harmless fantasy
And dreaming of romantasy.

So lost in reverie, she pined
But Burt was out in Hollywood
Too far to do her bad or good;

A stand-in she would have to find.
I said her fantasy was cute
And then agreed to stubstitute.

Passes Are Passé

"Men seldom makes passes
At girls who wear glasses" (Dorothy Parker)
Is as false as rose-colored snow
But women make asses
Of men who make passes
Whether with glasses or no.

The Rock

Through trials, torment, toil, and strife
A pillar of strength I would be for my wife
A rock that she can lean upon
No matter how badly things go wrong.

Now being a rock is hard enough
But my wife makes it doubly tough
I'm a hunk of marble, the way I plan it
—She keeps taking me for granite.

Cool Kiss

Don't kiss me, if that's all there is
Casual kissing makes me nervous
A kiss without serious intent
Is merely giving lip service.

This Bugs Me

In my garden as I tend and toil
To wrest a crop from the rocky soil
I watch the insects that buzz or run
And note a curious phenomenon;
Of lady bugs there are an awful lot
That populate my little garden plot
Yet though I search each squash and bean
Not a gentleman bug have I ever seen.
I wonder what did the lady do
That can be understood by me and you?
What could she have done in her buggly way
To make the gentlemen bugs go away?
Did she talk too much or clam up tight?
Fail to love him when the time was right?
Did she earn too much or squander his pay?
Spend all her time on ERA?
Did she cause him stress? Was she cold in bed?
Did he have to eat "out" when he had to be fed?
I haven't a clue to this mister-ee
'Cause my mind doesn't work like a bug's, you see.
And where does the male bug go when he goes?
To some hideaway bar where the bug juice flows?
Or does he just disappear in air that is thin
Leaving no trace in the place he has been?
There's nary a clue, still *I* haven't a doubt
He probably just died and took the sneaky way out.

Odds

He likes to save money
She likes to spend it
She makes conversation
He decides to end it.
What are the chances
True love will come alive?
About one in a thousand and five.

She likes her champagne
He prefers a beer
He wants a family
She pursues a "career."
What are the chances
That a baby will arrive?
About one in a thousand and five.

It's the battle of the sexes
That's fought right here at home
That's why so many exes
Are lonely and alone.
You may think me pessimistic
But time alone will tell
Odds that they'll not be a statistic
Are about the same as for a snowball in Hell.

She likes to travel
He's a stay-at-home
He's a letter writer
She always grabs the phone.
What are the chances
That this marriage will survive?
About one in a thousand and five.

When the Honeymoon Is Over

How does one really know
When the honeymoon is over?
Oh! there are many ways
But this one way
I know for certain.
The honeymoon is over
When your everlasting lover
Says, "Later, come back later."
Now, you may have heard the saying
"You can't keep a good man down"
But once he's totally destroyed
And lost his throne and crown
He will not easily arise
Although the occasion may;
His ego and incentive's gone
He's had a ruined day.
"How long did it last?" you ask.
Two months, seventeen days
Four hours, twenty-two minutes past.
"Not much of a record," you say.
No, but a pretty fair average, I'd bet
—So who cares for long honeymoons?
Love's promise awaits to be met!

Travel Talk

I can almost see the scene
With my keen imagination
I can recognize the characters
And hear the conversation;
Adam and Eve in Eden
And there amid the bliss
Eve is scolding Adam
And it sounds a lot like this.
"You never take me anyplace
At home we always stay;
Let's go someplace, most anyplace
Just to get away!"
"Honey, we're *in paradise,*"
Says Adam, soft and low;
"We're here in the Garden of Eden
Where *could* one want to go?"
At that Eve loses patience
And replies emphatically,
"You just don't want to go at all
Leastwise not with me.
No place on earth is calling you
And Heaven's safe as well;
You want to know where you can go?
—Well, you can go to Hell!!!"

One Phone Call?

I don't know if I'm legally married
A technicality may have set in;
I don't know if I should feel marital bliss
Or be merely miserable, living in sin.

Oh, the license was duly and properly signed
All officially issued and sealed;
The preacher presided, our vows we recited
The bells in the steeple were pealed.

Still, I don't know if I'm legally married
After years of smiles, love, and tears;
There's a loophole that looms ever larger
Beclouding my dreams and my fears.

Was I legally stripped of my freedom?
Was I entitled to marital delights?
Call out the judge and the jury
—Nobody read me my rights!

The Winner

I want to be fair and aboveboard
With the lady to whom I'm wed
Wouldn't think of taking advantage
I'll be upright and honest instead.

Still, in spite of my good intentions
(And I don't cheat or steal from her purse)
I know that I got the *best* of her
When she took me "for better or worse."

Be Prepared

The preacher's words were clear to me—
To prepare ourselves for eternity
We must learn the lessons that Jesus taught
As we travel life's path, with perils fraught.
We must learn to love and turn the cheek
Be gentle and kind in the way we speak;
We must sacrifice and learn to share
Most massive burdens choose to bear;
We must make a commitment and follow through
Show concern for others in all we do;
This is a start and there's much, much more
To prepare us for knocking on that heavenly door.
Though I may be wrong, I feel I'm way ahead
I gained most of the above by just being wed.

Because

It's oft been said that love is blind
That people who profess it
When asked, can very seldom find
What caused them to express it
But you and I, my turtledove
Comprise a case unique.
Though reasons for our tender love
We've had no need to seek
A hundred, yes, a thousand
Could I name for loving you:
I love you, 'cause I love you, 'cause . . .
Well, just because I do.

Bedtime Story

When my wife is feeling restless
In a night of turn and toss
There's just no chance for sleeping
Is the night a total loss?

No! I don't mind her restless movements
Won't let them drive me to distraction
I just go with the flow, ride with the tide
—And hope for a piece of the action.

Marital Semi-Bliss

Nothing there is that can compare
A loving wife, her husband's care.
When at the hard-won close of day
I homeward wend my weary way
Her greeting lends a cheery note
She helps take off my overcoat
Embeds me in an easy chair
And brings my pipe and slippers there.
As I enjoy my sweet repose
She puts my glasses on my nose
The evening paper in my hand
And softly on the radio she tunes my favorite band;
In short, she's just the sweetest wife
    A fellow ever had—
And then she talks and talks and talks
    And nearly drives me *mad*.

Helpmates

A devoted do-it-yourselfer
I do all by myself that I can;
I write my own poems, sing my own songs
I'm even my own garbageman.
I change my own oil, pump my own gas
Even replace my spark plugs and yet
Anytime that it's time to make love
I take all the help I can get.

And you're the one I want to help me
Without you, my love's on the shelf;
With your help, love's all that it should be
So help me, I can't help myself.

I paint and I paper my kitchen
Lay carpet and tile wall to wall
I was even my own electrician
Till the union man paid me a call.
Whenever my lawn needs mowing
I can do it myself with no sweat
But whenever it's time to make love
I want all the help I can get!
HELP!

The Storyteller

A man in his life, if he has a wife
Gets called a lot of things
And most, you can bet, he'd rather forget
And some can give his heart wings.
I've been called "real great," "too little, too late"
And some words that I can't spell
But she gave *me* the label "Ol' Tom T"
For the stories that I tell.

Now you married guys will realize
Marriage is some kind of thing
And a wife makes perpetual winter
Or brings everlasting spring.
Though I've been called a drunk, a shiftless skunk
And a turtle without a shell
I'm proudest that *she* called me "Ol' Tom T"
For the stories that I tell.

When I come home late from a heavy date
A story is my only hope;
A convenient lie with another standin' by
If she says, "Now, I'm no dope."
She might call me fickle or an ol' dill pickle
Dirty pup or a hound of Hell
But it's the greatest when *she* calls me "Ol' Tom T"
For the stories that I tell.
I love it when *she* calls me "Ol' Tom T"
For the stories that I tell;
I've got it made when *she* calls me "Ol' Tom T"
For the stories . . .

Seems Like Forever

The subject of discussion was
"What makes a marriage last?"
Responses from the audience
Were coming thick and fast;
Still the answers weren't conclusive
No one had the bottom line
A philosophy of marriage
That would stand the test of time.
Then up stood Ol' George Farnham
And the crowd grew hushed and still
"If anyone can bring us truth
Then Ol' George Farnham will."
Ol' George has been "much married"
But only to one wife
So we thought he'd have the formula
For long-lasting married life.
Ol' George slowly cleared his throat
He suffered no stage fright
His wife could not suppress his words
She wasn't there that night.
He said, "What makes a man hang in
(And it holds him like a curse)
Is the knowing if he tried again
That he could do much worse.
And the reason that a woman stays?
Her pride won't let her tell
Her friends and all the neighbors
That she didn't marry well.
That she's got a rotten husband
To the world she will not say
—But she doesn't mind reminding *him*
Every single day!"

Hear, Hear!

When I said that I am a listener
Some of you snickered and smiled
You feel that I may be stretching the truth
And I *do* get a little bit wild.
Still, I think I'm basically honest
That I've ne'er lost the listener's touch
I've had plenty of practice at listening
Because—I've been married so much!

One Never Knows

If she says, "you're an animal," beware
She may not be seeing a tiger there.
A lion, perhaps? Well, maybe, but then
Her "animal" may vary time and again.

If you're in the doghouse a lot, you're a dog
In a classy café she may think you a hog;
If running away has oft been your habit
In her eyes you may be more like a rabbit.
Be certain that you behave so that
The animal she means—is not an ape or rat;
You think that "animal" may mean you're a "hunk"
But in her mind it may be a jackass or skunk.

There are so many possibilities here
At best, we can only hope she means "deer."

Advice to Single Ladies

If you're waiting for "Mr. Right"
And expect him on a white
Horse, ashine with his armor agleam
Don't choose a mere mortal man.
Even doing the best he can
He will never live up to your dream.

Let him happily go his way;
To urge or tempt him to stay
Would mean marital "Hell to pay"

Nor yet for a man by your side
Choose one with your eyes open wide
Whose faults are apparent to all

Believing that after "I do"
You'll remake him to suit only you
Till his flaws are incredibly small.
If either thought enters your mind
Stay single—you surely will find
You have blest all of mankind.

Yet still, if you really *must* wed
Remove all thoughts from your head
Of finding a "perfect" man;
Accept one "as is" and rejoice.
Though he be not the "perfect" choice
He'll do the best that he can
To be what you want him to be
While being *himself;* you see
No one is "perfect," not even thee
No one—not even thee.

My Keeper

Yes, I said, "my wife and keeper"
And before I get in deeper
Perhaps it would be best if I explain—
She keeps my life in order
And she keeps our loving strong;
She keeps me well and happy
Here at home where I belong;
She keeps me well-nutritioned
And also in clean clothes;
She keeps me feeling thankful
And she keeps me on my toes;
She keeps me in affection
With sweet kisses by the score;
She keeps me feeling loved
And she keeps me wanting more.

Caution—No Lock!

If someone else should try the door
While you're still on the seat
Just grab the knob with both your hands
And, yes! do brace your feet;
Then scream a lot and you will not
Be molested any more.
Now is that too darn much trouble
To save us buyin' a bolt for the door?

Singles-Bar Encounter

I met this guy in Jerry's Bar
We joined in conversation
He said that he'd come, oh, so far
We should have a celebration.
I'm a lady who knows her way about
I didn't fall for his line
As I left him there, I had no doubt
When he said he wanted "peace of mind"
He was after a "piece of mine."

Fire Extinguisher (Gift)

When he's just too, TOO romantic
And you're just not in the mood
No need to conjure up a headache
Or to lock the door and brood.

When you see raw, naked passion
Like a dancer on a wire
Grab this handy little gizmo
And extinguate the fire!!

Nuts to———

By means both honest and also quite fair
Several bushels of nuts I acquired;
I would crack nuts religiously every day
Till my arm and my back would get tired.

Now, it happens my disposition is mild
Easygoing and peaceful my mien
And all these unrelated conditions
Brought a smile to the local scene.

My friends had reason to chide me
Saying ladies all down the street
When referring to me in their chatter
Now call me "The Nutcracker, Sweet."

Social Standing

A birthday present from my wife
Has greatly changed my social life;
In that bright birthday interlude
To make of me a well-dressed dude
A three-piece suit she gave.

Now, invitations do I get
From ladies I have never met
Inviting me to be a guest
At festive functions, all the best.
I don't know why or give a hoot, they add,
"Do come in your birthday suit."

Yuppie

They say that the day of the "hippy" is past
That "yuppies" prevail now, both hard and fast;
The "baby-boomers" who have come of age
Have purloined a position at center stage.

Though I'm *more* than a generation apart
I must be a "yuppie" deep in my heart.
When my wife asks.
"Will you do this, you miserable pup?"
My only and always answer is "Yup."

"Never Mind, I'll Do It Myself"

I'd like to help in the kitchen
When my wife is preparing a meal;
A couple working together
Seems a situation ideal.
But I've trouble recalling procedures
That makes conditions much worse; "Uh,
Do I peel nuts and chop the potatoes?
Or vice versa?"

She'd Better Not

There's a double standard in my life
That's causing a problem twixt me and my wife.
A night out with the *boys*
Is one of my special joys;
She says, "Two can play at that game."
But she knows that I'd brood
Come completely unglued
If *she* should try doing the same.

Part VII

Philosophy—Religion—the Church

The author has at times been charged with having a lighthearted view of religion and church affairs. On the contrary, he is quite serious in believing that everyone is free to have their own beliefs and that there is a positive and stabilizing role in our world of today for "lukewarm" Christians, as opposed to fanatics.

Partners

Oh, God can make the garden grow
No matter what we plant or sow;
He sends the sun and brings the rain
Till all is flower, fruit, and grain.

But look! the weeds are growing, too
And bugs and worms creep in like dew;
All has been done to no avail
God's crop is surely doomed to fail.

But wait! disaster may be stayed.
Though naught can I without His aid
It's plain enough for all to see
—God needs a lot of help from *me*.

Raising youths is like that, too
We try our very best to do
The things that make them thrive and grow
And teach them what they ought to know.

We do our best to spare them pain
Steer clear of pitfalls to us plain;
Help them to walk where shame won't trod
—*We* need a lot of help from God.

Late Spring Snow

It came soft and uninvited
Tiptoeing in like sleep;
When darkness slipped away at dawn
The snow was white and deep.

All through the night it surely fell
White blanketing the ground;
No warning thunder echoed
It came without a sound.

Falling straight from Heaven
Unswept by any breeze
It put a furry overcoat
On wires, lines, and trees.

And if it hadn't come at all
It's beauty we'd miss, no doubt
Though it was high up on the list
Of things we could do without.

Harbinger

The wind was cold and bitter
It snowed like everything
But birds began to twitter
And some began to sing.
I walked by a pussy willow
A friendly, furry thing
I talked to a pussy willow
It promised me—a spring.

Snow Job

It's hard to believe that those downy flakes
As they come drifting down on the land and lakes
To blanket the forests, the fields, and the prairie
Are each crafted uniquely by God or a fairy
So no two are ever exactly alike
But are always as different as Pat is from Mike.

Who did the research? what were his credentials?
Was the study extensive or just bare essentials?
How many trillions of flakes were perused
Before a conclusion was finally conclused?
And what of the flakes that fall in the ocean?
Does anyone know or have any notion
If, perhaps, one of them might perfectly match
A flake from Fredonia or Lower Dogpatch?

Yet still the flakes sift on silently down
With nary a care, a worry, a frown—
Unconcerned that our survey is flawed and aware
That the final results are still up in the air.

Piddle Paddle*

Keep this with you constantly
—You'll never lose the battle;
Know that you will never be
—Up the creek without a paddle.

*A tiny, hand-whittled wooden paddle was presented to each family member along with this verse.

Versatile Love

We love blueberry muffins
And we love to roller skate;
We love a horse or puppy
And we love to stay up late.

Of course, we love our siblings
But not like man and wife;
We love our friends and families
As much as we love life.

We are filled with love of country
And that patriotic zeal
Is a very different loving
From the love of God we feel.

From the Bible's "Love thy neighbor"
To "sweet love and charity"
This overworked yet willing word
May save humanity.

If we love "love" so very much
Perhaps *love* will come to be;
There should be love for everyone
Especially—you and me!

The Censors

These self-appointed guardians of the morals of mankind
Found themselves convened, in a crusading frame of mind.
They decided that the only way to keep the language clean
Was to banish all four-letter words, "They're evil and
    obscene."
So how to go about it was the next thing to discuss
How best to abrogate them with the leastest fuss and muss;
Some favored banishment at once from every new edition
While others leaned toward "slow but sure," the process of
    attrition;
Then someone spoke, with wisdom going far beyond his
    years,
"Let's get them all together and we'll ask for volunteers;
Then we won't have to pick and choose and when we're
    finally done
They'll all be gone, like smoke rings they'll have vanished
    one by one."
Agreed—and so they brought them in and stood them all
    around
The spokesman told them what was planned, you couldn't
    hear a sound
And when he asked who'd be the first to *not* be anymore
'Twas "LOVE" that rose so softly and tiptoed out the door.

Let's Not Forget
(Written especially for Organ Dedication and Homecoming Day of the Otego United Methodist Church.)

If you ask anyone in my hometown,
"Where's the Methodist church?" They'll send you down
To a neat white building on a quiet street
Where the sill is well-worn by passing feet
And a Welcome is posted before the same
Listing times of worship and our pastor's name.
But—the building alone is an empty shell.
No melodious chords will peal and swell
From the organ, the choir, or the congregation;
No powerful prayers for the world and the nation
Will implore our God, unless *we* are there
To join in the hymns, the message, the prayer.
We are apt to to forget from time to time—
Not the organ, the pulpit, nor even the chime
Neither stained-glass windows nor spirelike steeple
Are a church. The church is the people
Who meet on Sunday and day by day
Endeavor to live in a Christian way.
The church is the children who romp through the door
And all of the souls that have gone before;
The pastor, the parish, the worshippers all
Who come in answer to a personal call.

We are fond of our church home, our organ, and yet
We are the church—let's not forget.

Lay Leader?
You've Got to Be Kidding!

I appreciate the great honor
Which on me you'd like to bestow
But I've never sought after high office
For reasons that you should know.

There are some things in my history
I wouldn't want brought to light
Like the way that I teased my sisters
Or that I once wet the bed at night.

And you surely can find a witness
That I've sometimes told a crude joke
That wouldn't stand up to the scrutiny
Of prim, pious, prudish folk.

If revealing "all of the above"
Wouldn't keep me out of the show
In addition, I guess I'm a "yes man"
'Cause I find it so hard to say *no*.

I feel that it's best to confess
Than face charges brought up later
And find myself in a mess
Of allegations by some allegator.

Now we know that present-day candidates
Must be perfect, with nary a flaw
And so now—my nomination
I respectfully do withdraw.

Tongue-in-Cheek Organ Fund Plea
or
Who's Gonna Pay so the Organ Can Play?

When I needed transportation
I bought a well-used car
And while I paid and paid and paid
It took me long and far.

When I bought a motorcycle
The dealer took *me* for a ride;
Before I ever rode the cycle
He didn't break me—but he tried.

I bought a house and furniture
Just so I'd have a home;
No one ever helped *me* pay
I did it all alone.

For things I ride or drive or own
I always have to pay;
That was determined long ago
It's the great American way.

I'll pay for *my* things as long as I live
And longer if *they* can contrive it;
So—let the organist pay for the organ
She's the only one who will drive it.

Organ Fund Plea

We do need your organ donations
But we don't ask for kidney or liver
We just ask that you give from the heart
"God loveth a cheerful giver."

Don't Count Me Out, Lord
(A hymn poem.)

Lord, you know just where to find me
Sinner that I am;
I'm depending on your mercy
To bring me to the Lamb.

[*Chorus*]
Don't count me out, Lord
I want to belong
But don't count me in
Till I've finished my song.

Often I have felt you near me
Known your saving Grace;
I believe that you will hear me
And meet me face to face.

[*Repeat Chorus*]
Don't reveal when you'll be calling
To take my very soul;
Likely, I will kick and struggle
When you call the roll.

[*Repeat Chorus*]
I'd linger yet with those who love me
With those I love so well;
Then, perhaps, I'll be more ready
To say my last farewell.

[*Repeat Chorus*]

Healthy, Wealthy, and Wise

Old sayings, maxins, proverbs
Have value still today
When answers we are seeking
They are there to point the way;
To lead to proper action
In these times of strain and stress
Like "Cast your bread upon the waters"
And you'll have a soggy mess.
"Saving for a rainy day"
Is for some other fella
Unless, of course, we're saving
A good waterproof umbrella.
If the course is at a snail's pace
Then "Slow and steady wins the race."
"A penny saved is a penny urned"
When we store it in a vase.
"There's no fool like an old fool"
Yet a young one is just as unique
And a six-foot depth of God's good earth
Will be "inherited by the meek."
"Don't look a gift horse in the mouth"
On that we can depend
And if that horse is heading South
Don't peep in the north end.
"The early bird will catch the worm"
Means naught until I see—
Am I equated with the bird?
Or could the worm be me?
For the wisdom of the ages
May be couched in simple terms
If we only can determine
Which are birds, and who are worms.

On Reincarnation

The devil said, "You're goin' home
Back from whence you came;
You left an earthly place to come
You go back to the same.
Just one more thing, you're gonna be
A vegetable this time;
You choose the one you want to be
—It has to fit my rhyme.
So would you be a pumpkin
A tomato, squash, or beet
A cucumber or a carrot
Or a pepper, hot or sweet?"
I quickly did some thinking
And I said, "I'll be a bean
Not a lima, string, or kidney
Not a yellow nor a green.
A *human* bean', I'll settle for
That's all I'll be," said I.
The devil found a lonely spot
Where he could sob and cry.

The Malpractice Suers

If I should die, I'll go below;
It's true we reap just what we sow
And though the fault be mine alone
Instead of trying to atone
I'll start a huge malpractice suit
(You know I'm mean enough to do it)
Against the pastor of my church
For leaving me in sinful lurch
—Unfit to answer Heaven's bell
Yet eminently unprepared for Hell.

Some devilish lawyer for a helluva fee
Will crucify to win for me.
He'll surely smear that preacher's name
To make sure someone shares the blame
For leaving me without a prayer
At the time for climbing the golden stair.

So preachers, select with the utmost care
The clients you choose for salvation there
Lest you be cited for malpractice and fraud
In failing to bring a soul to GOD
While the lawyers of Hell, in roses and clover
Will sue and sue—till it freezes over.

Speaking of Words

> *A man with nothing to say has no words. Can its reverse be true—A man who has no one to say anything to, has no words as he has no need for words?*
> —John Steinbeck
>   *Travels with Charley in Search of America*

Wrong! We still need words, I say
We've a need to speak them every day
To tell ourselves that we've sometimes strayed
To humble ourselves when "we've got it made"
To defend ourselves when we're too severe
To put in perspective things not too clear
To remind ourselves that we must forgive
That the world may be changed by the way we live
To say a thank you for blessings at hand
To ask for help with the things we've planned.

It's not that I talk to myself, you see
—It's a conversation twixt God and me.

Seldom Pray-er
(In tribute to the many "lukewarm" Christians.)

I'm turning to you in crisis, Lord
And asking your help for me.
Not that I'm especially worthy, Lord
—I'm unworthy as I can be.
Nor am I especially faithful
—"Sinner" best describes me.
Still, I believe you will listen
And answer my desperate call
If only because it's been ever so long
Since I've asked for a thing at all.

"For Whom the Bell Tolls"

In days of my youth
I cared little for truth
As preached by prophets of old;
I worried, not much
Of salvation and such
Or being a sheep of the fold.

Still, on each Sunday morn
In spite of my scorn
To the church I sped swiftly and well
'Cause for two years or more
They gave me the chore
Of ringing that beautiful bell.

Like a carrot to a rabbit
That bell gave me the habit
Of being each week in my pew
And from point of no hope
Just pulling that rope
Taught me all the religion I knew.

So if sermons and singing
And prayers and hand wringing
Can't deter me from fires of Hell,
Perhaps, in those times
Of the harps and the chimes
I still may be—"saved by the bell."

With Love

Everyone loves a butterfly
Its beauty is plain to all
But the poor little worm
That the butterfly was

Everyone loves a handsome prince
As he smiles, standing strong and tall
But the toad on the road
To becoming that prince
Hardly got any love at all.

Everyone loves a lovely bride
In her radiance, wall to wall
But that crying babe
Twenty years ago
Hardly got any love at all.

Everyone loves a butterfly
Its beauty is plain to all
But the poor little worm
That the Butterfly was
Hardly got any love at all.

[*Postlude*]
Let's give *everyone* all the love that we can
Not save it for only some;
With the help of that love
By the Grace of God
How lovable we each may become.

Gardening

'Most every day I can be found
Out in my garden just "puttering 'round."
That's what I do, so I've been told
But that's a view that I don't hold.
Last week God watered my garden twice
Even once would have been quiet nice
Between the showers He sent sunshine
To encourage and nurture these seeds of mine.

Now, I'll be durned if I can see
Why God should "putter 'round" with me
When He's such important things to do
And still be the Lord of Creation, too.

Unless it could be that tilling the ground
Is a whole lot more than—just "puttering 'round."

Forest Cathedral
(Crumhorn Mountain Scout Camp)

I've heard tall tales of talking trees
I've been in a forest alone;
There was silence there, except for the breeze
Solitude born of wood and stone.
The whispering pines murmured not at all
The quiet of calm was complete;
The arboreal chapel was spacious and tall
Stretching skyward toward God's holy feet.
If any tree spoke on the trail that I trod
It was a sound heard only by God.

Destiny

We cannot know nor can we
Even yet pretend to understand
What life can hold or time unfold
Unknown what God has planned.

Who of us all will still remain
In torment, travail, pain, and doubt?
And who will be the chosen few
Whose candle flickers swiftly out?

In truth, each one has a course to run—
You have yours and I have mine—
And whether we sprint or jog or plod
—God determines the finish line.

Aquatic Flight
(Crumhorn Mountain Scout Camp)

We're flying—
Moving swift and low
Our altitude is constant
And softly as we go
We see the beauty
Of the lake, the woods, the sky.
The water as it pat—pat—pats our bottom
Transmits its gentle strength to us
Granting its support, not asking why.
Complexities of daily care
Disappear in clear pure air
As our paddles dip and flash
And our canoe glides swiftly by.

Reverend Dodson

I once had the sorrowful obligation
Of saying "Good-bye" for a whole congregation
To a minister who'd been a favorite of all
As he left to answer another call.
For more years than we'd care to tell
His devotion and wisdon had served us well . . .
As I sought to soften the parting pain
With memorable words that would remain
I said, "Old friends are like old shoes—
Letting them go gives one the blues."

Then the reverend replied,
"Old friends *are* like old shoes, no doubt
For the simple reason, they're both worn out."
It occurred to me then that this gentle man
Had given us all that a prophet can
Had worn himself out for humanity
For friends, church, family, and community.
And he'd given us faith that he'd give much more;
This, for him, was another open door
Another chance to serve and share
Another place for "old shoes" to wear.

Seven Best Buys

The sun in the morning
And the moon at night
The love we give to others
Honest, steady toil
The best health one can enjoy
Refreshing sleep, with sweet dreams blest.
When these no longer bring one joy—
Then death.

Ordinary People
(Miss Virginia O'Malley spoke on this topic in her first sermon in our church.)

"Ordinary People" was the topic
Of the pastor's Sunday sermon.
Well, *that* is every one of us
From what I can determine.

If assembled like an auto
We'd have a "people" basic model
Then "extras" would start adding on
By the time we'd start to toddle.

God's special gifts and blessings
Extra strength or speed or power
Extra-ordinary brilliance
Gifts that cause us each to flower.

But in the eyes of our Creator
From the moment each awoke
We're one birth, one life, one death
In short, just ordinary folk.

Lincoln said, "Ordinary people
Surely god must love them
Else why in Heaven's name
Would He have made so many of them?"

Retiring Church Organist

It will never be the same
And we never shall forget
Florence, as she played the organ.
We can hear those anthems yet.

For we hardly can remember
When she *wasn't* playing there
As we came as youths to worship
Or, in the choir, we climbed the stair.

All our lives are filled with memories
Of those golden, happy years
As her music swelled with passion
Or inspired us to tears.

And the glory of that music
Lured our growing girls and boys
To come, to pray, to worship
And to make a joyful noise.

As you leave the keyboard, Florence
To another's skillful touch
We would share this gentle tribute
With one we love so much—

We hope the years have brought *you*
Many lovely memories, too
As we say, "Good luck, God bless you
And all happiness to you."

The Bridge Builder*
(By Will Allen Dromgoole)

An old man, going a lone highway
Came at the evening, cold and gray
To a chasm, vast and deep and wide
Through which was flowing a sullen tide.
The old man crossed in the twilight dim—
That sullen stream had no fears for him,
But he turned, when he reached the other side
And built a bridge to span the tide.

"Old man," said a fellow traveler near,
"You are wasting strength in building here.
Your journey will end with the ending day.
You never again must pass this way.
You have crossed the chasm, deep and wide,
Why build you the bridge at the eventide?"

The builder lifted his old gray head.
"Good friend, in the path I have come," he said
"There followeth after me today
A youth whose feet must pass this way.
This chasm that has been naught to me
To that fair-haired youth may a pitfall be.
He too, must cross in the twilight dim;
Good friend, I am building the bridge for him."

*Surely the excellence of this poem deserves a sequel, however medicore; see following page.

The Apprentice
(Sequel to "The Bridge Builder" by Will Allen Dromgoole.)

The bridge builder finished building his bridge
And then crossed over to watch from the ridge.
The fair-haired youth was not long coming
But on the way he'd done some slumming.
He was unkempt and disheveled
And likely as not
He had paused on the way to smoke some pot.
A motley crew he had gathered 'round
And the canyon echoed with their fury and sound.
"Who built this bridge without our permission?
Whoever he was, may he rot in perdition.
Ecology has been damaged here
(Throw the cans in the canyon
When we've finished the beer)."

The bridge builder smiled in his knowing way
"He's young and foolish, but there'll come a day
He'll appreciate the toil and the care
The love that, made a bridge for him there.
God grant him the wisdom, as *his* twilight nears
To become the bridge builder of future years."

Hot and Cold

I had this dream that I had died
And straight to Hell I went.
The first few days in greeting friends
And relatives I spent.
The weather was so nice and warm
It really was a treat;
No one was suffering shivery chills
Or frozen ears or feet.
I thought, *Oh, this is Heaven*
No place like it anywhere
I'll ask the one in charge if there's
A room that he can spare.
Then as I went in search to find
The great perdition petitioner
Some SOB of low degree
Turned on the air conditioner. -*&/*

Sequel to "Hot and Cold"

I've given this a lot of thought—
With Yankee ingenuity
And governmental screwity
A pipeline surely could be built;
Bring all that heat, as warm as toast
Right up here where we need it most.
Of course, it'd cost an awful lot—
Several trillion dollars worth—
But we'd be, oh, so warm and cozy
With our Hell right here on earth.

Christmas Reflections

For Christmas this year let's spread Christmas cheer
With gifts that money can't buy;
The things that we give in the way that we live
May be treasures in somebody's eye.

To our neighbors and friends
Let's give smiles without end
And a cheery "Hello" when we meet
And love will mean more in a neighborly chore
Or homemade gastronomical treat.

We might shovel some snow or offer to hoe
Or give beans or jelly or sauce;
Things that show caring, a spirit of sharing
So dear yet to us no great loss.

With gifts from the heart, we might even start
A trend that could spread far and near;
Then before we are through, it could even be true
That Christmas *might* last the whole year.

Gift List—for My Friends

Instead of traditional gifts this year
I'm giving service and labor
So if you need a hand or a handyman
Call on me, your friendly neighbor.
Like if your auto won't go
It turns over too slow
You can't figure what can the matter be;
Just call R-A-Y and to you I will fly
So happy to charge up your battery.

Christmas Spirit

We often like to think
Of the good old-fashioned days
When we celebrated Christmas
In less-sophisticated ways
And yet when we remember
That a Babe was born in love
Things haven't changed so very much
The same stars shine above.
While rushing, working, hurrying
The busy season through
That Babe helps us remember
His love is our love, too.

Just Naturally Neighborly

There are times, I profess
When it's right to say yes
Sometimes it's best to say no;
The decision is frequently fraught with stress.
How *is* a person to know?
I always say yes if I possibly can
To matters of life, love, and labor;
Who wouldn't want to be known as a man
Who never says neigh to a neighbor?

An Offertory Parady: How Long Has It Been?

How long has it been
Since you put some cash in?
How long since the plate knew your token?
How long since you paid
On that pledge that you made?
How long since your money has spoken?

How long has it been
Since you paid for your sin
Or made a down payment on Heaven?
Take your dough from that sack
Don't hold a thing back
Invest in a life that is new;
It will surely do wonders for *you.*

Biblical Logic

My mind keeps seeking logic
While I'm trying to believe
What the preachers say is *gospel*
In the stories that they weave
Of other times, other places
Lessons from the long ago
Of other countries, peoples, races.

Still some things change but little
As the moon and stars, remember?
Could it be the *burning bush*
Was just a sumac in September?

To a Beloved Pastor and Family

"Parting is such sweet sorrow"
Wrote the Bard long years ago.
Will we find the sweetness tomorrow
In fond memory's afterglow?

How can we properly bid farewell
To a family who from us departs?
Friends we have loved not long but well
Who have found their way into our hearts.

We offer "Best wishes" and a tearful "Good-bye,
May God bless you in all you endeavor."
Six years went by in the blink of an eye
When we wanted to have you forever.

A Weak Sinner's Prayer for Strength

Lord, please keep the things I covet
So high, I can't reach them;
Help the women to run so fast
I can't catch them;
And please, Lord
Make me work so hard
And so much
That when the devil invites me
To join him for fun and games
I'll be
1) too busy, 2) too tired, 3) sound asleep.

Let's Face It

At my age
There's bound to be a few wrinkles
On my brow, my face, and my tummy.
Does it worry me? Nah!
Not really at all;
I'm aging but I'm not a dummy.

In youth I accepted the *who* that I was
I accept what now I've become;
If wrinkles are part of the picture
So be it—it bothers me none.

Whatever I've been or am to be
Evolves from God-given gifts.
Wrinkles and all, you'll often find me
In church—for my weekly faith lifts.

Think about It

I listened to the preacher
And stored my treasures high;
Not here on earth, you understand
In that big storehouse in the sky.

Now that my life and spirit are gone
Somebody's doing well
Enjoying my earthly treasures
While I'm sweating here in Hell.

One Man Awake

One man awake
Can waken another;
The second wakens
His next-door brother;
The three awake
Can rouse the town
By turning the whole place
Upside down;

The many awake
Can make such a fuss
That it finally wakens
The rest of us.

One man up
With dawn in his eyes
Multiplies.

One Man Awake Parody

From "One Man Awake" in "For Heaven's Sake" as used in teachers' guide for Explore, Methodist Sunday school material, author unknown.

One man awake
Can waken his mate
And between them
Neither can sleep;
To read, it's too late
No good to count sheep
The tv is is out
And there's nothing about
To amuse or to entertain.

One man awake
Who doesn't arise
Multiplies.

Oh, My Soul and Body

During much of my time on earth
They said I was out of my mind;
I thought I was fairly normal
Just being—"one of a kind."

Now, soon they say I may see Heaven
Where all is angelic and Godly
But what I must do to get there
Is just to—get out of my body.

It takes body and soul
To make me feel whole
And my mind is wondering whether
It's the right thing to do
To separate the two
That have been all these years together.

Reincar-notion?

Now, you've convinced me that I can come back
In some other time and place
As some other person in some other body
Wearing somebody's else's face.

So knowing I'll have another bona fide chance
To live a life, sweet, simple, and uncomplexed
Wouldn't it be wise to total what's left
Of *this* life? *and get on with the next*!

Garden Story

Adam and Eve in the garden did err
Then they found that they needed clothes.
Adam got some coveralls along with shoes and hose.
He said, "Thank God, I needed those;
The other night I almost froze."
Eve fashioned filmy negligee
Designed just right to tease;
She said, "What will the neighbors say
When I put lace on these?"

Another Garden Story

Adam and Eve in the garden did err
Stolen fruit made somebody a thief;
They clothed themselves there in leaves of the fig
That's when Adam—turned over a new leaf.

Fitting Footwear

I wear ski boots when I'm skiing
When I'm skating, I'm in skates
Work shoes are for working
Dress shoes are for dates
Loafers are for loafing
When I jog, I'm wearing Jox
And I hear the Sunday sermon
In my holiest of socks.

Between Anthems

Up in the choir loft, from this lofty perch
I pensively ponder. How come
A *pew* means a very "bad" smell
Or a very "good" seat in the church?

How Do I remember My Age?*

How do I remember my age? It's easy—
My age consists of two digits.
The first digit is twice the second digit.
The sum of the two digits, divided by the second digit equals the second digit.
The sum of the two digits also equals the number of my grandchildren.
The sum of the two digits multiplied by infinity equals the number of
My blessings, for which I am grateful and give thanks to God.

*This I thought of in church, so it should be pretty *good*. It's been several years since I discovered this formula and each year a new formula is born to make the figures fit my age. Can *you* solve the equation? It also reveals the number of my grandchildren.

Recipe for One Small Choir
(By a choir member who knows.)

Take two parts soprano
A smidgeon of alto
Add one heaping portion of bass
Fold in one level measure of tenor
Mix until thoroughly confused
Heat in the ecclesiastical oven
Until half-baked.

Part VIII

Love Songs and a Few Others

Most of the material in this category was written to be sung, and in fact, though musical notes have never been put to paper, there are tunes for most of them in the author's head and on tape. I do not subscribe to the modern contention that lyrics are not important and that "no one listens to the words." Of course, a masterful marriage of music and lyrics is the ideal, yet in many instances the lyrics *are* the song.

My Love Songs

When I first started writing
I was just a kid in school
Some folks said I was literary
Some said I was a fool
But I early learned to realize
The beauty that's in words
Long, long before I knew about
The honey bees and birds.
Then I kept my pen in practice
Writing classroom notes and jokes
And I started writing letters
To my friends and all my folks
And quite a few nice ladies
Had some poems that were mine
But none of them could ever claim
To be my Valentine.

[*Chorus*]
I wrote all my love songs to you
I sang all my love songs to you
When my songs are no more sung
And I've reached the final rung
Of life's ladder
These words will still be true—
I wrote all my love songs to you.

Long, Long Ago*

[*Verse 1*]
I have some bills that were due long ago
Long, long ago; long, long ago
How I can pay them, I really don't know
Really don't know, I don't know
The car payment's due and I can't let it pass
I floated a loan for ten gallons of gas
My paycheck is gone and I've nothing to show
But things that I bought long ago.

[*Verse 2*]
Do you remember the styles long ago
Long, long, ago; long, long ago
High necks and bustles and skirts to the toe
Yes, they were long, long ago
Ladies, permit us some tips on your clothes
Wear lots of minis with sheer pantyhose
Halters and bare backs and—anything goes
Help us forget the long ago.

[*Verse 3*]
We had some girl friends that we used to know
Long, long ago; long, long ago
Susie and Sally and Mary and Flo
We loved them so—long ago
Sweet, gentle memories still come and go
Years have gone by, but we hope they don't show
We can't love them all 'cause our wives told us so
Long, long ago, long ago.

*These revised lyrics were written to be sung to the tune "Long Long Ago," written long, long ago by Thomas Haynes Bayley. They have been used numerous times by my brother, Bob, and I, as we have sung in harmony for family or senior groups.

Good-bye, My Lover, Good-bye*

[*Verse 1*]
You ladies now may have your day
Good-bye, my lover, good-bye
They say you've come a long, long way
Good-bye, my lover, good-bye
You take our jobs throughout the day
Good-bye, my lover, good-bye
At night you're on the town to play
Good-bye, my lover, good-bye.

[*Chorus*]
By-low, my baby; by-low, my baby
By-low, my baby; good-bye, my lover, good-bye

[*Verse 2*]
You wear our pants, you're one with us
Good-bye, my lover, good-bye
You smoke our smokes, you drink and cuss
Good-bye, my lover, good-bye
The times must change is what you say
Good-bye, my lover, good-bye
We loved you more the other way
Good-bye, my lover, good-bye.

[*Chorus*]
By-low, my baby; by-low, my baby
By-low, my baby; good-bye, my lover, good-bye.

*These revised lyrics were written to be sung to the old, old classic, "Good-bye, My Lover, Good-bye," author unknown.

[*Verse 3*]
Oh, yes we loved you better then
Good-bye, my lover, good-bye
When girls were ladies instead of men
Good-bye, my lover, good-bye
You walked with flirty girlish charm
Good-bye, my lover, good-bye
Now combat boots your feet may warm
Good-bye, my lover, good-bye.

[*Chorus*]
By-low, my baby; by-low, my baby
By-low, my baby; good-bye, my lover, good-bye.

I Love You Just the Same

I never knew that love could so completely
Engulf me and drown me, oh, so sweetly
And I know we're not to blame
I knew that lovin' you was trouble
But I loved you just the same.

My heart has never known such ecstasy
I know our love is all that love can be
My happy heart admits no shame
I knew that lovin' you was trouble
But I loved you just the same.

I knew that my arms had to hold you
Your eyes reflect the tender love I told you;
I don't know if we're goin' anyplace
I love the love that's mirrored in your face.

I know I'm glad you came
I know that lovin' you is trouble
But I love you just the same:
I know that lovin' you is trouble
But I love you . . .

Windchill Loving

The very thought of you makes me high
Cloud nine is waiting there in the sky
Nothing can dampen my ardor, I know
Then your windchill factor gives me a LOW.

You arouse every bit of the love in my soul
There's an animal in me that I can't control
When you look at me, I become instant lover
Then your windchill factor drives me to cover.

I love your lips, your nose, your eyes
The way you make my thermometer rise
And then when I think that it just can't stop
Your windchill factor makes it drop
Your windchill factor lays me low.

Just to be near you makes me hot
Makes me want to love you with all I've got
But when I'm all ready—all systems are *"go"*—
Your windchill factor lays me low.

Now, I've done all right in the summer heat
Fahrenheit, Celsius, I can beat;
I'm still young enough, but I might grow old
While your windchill factor is leavin' me COLD.

Baby, What Am I Supposed to Do?

You say you've learned to get along without me
Well, that may all be very well for you
You promise that you'll never think about me
But, Baby, what am I supposed to do?

You tell yourself that you can soon forget me
No matter that my love is strong and true
You don't care if the gloomy blues do get me
But, Baby, what am I supposed to do?

My heart's computered to the magic of your charms
And I'm programmed just to hold you in my arms.

Well, now you say you've crossed me from your mind
Makes no difference that I only think of you
Your love was just the temporary kind
But, Baby, what am I supposed to do?

Think

Think of all the good times that we knew
You know that I'll be thinking of them, too;
No matter how we try
There's no way you and I
Can ever make a go of being through.

Think—is what I'm doin' Baby, now that we're apart
If only I'd been thinkin' then, I wouldn't have broke your heart;
My thoughts and dreams are all of you—and how I loved you then
I hope it's not too late for me to win you back again.

Think of how we had it yesterday
Just you and I together all the way;
Think of wasting all that moon above
And, darling, think of me—and please think love.

Love's Memories

The things that we've loved together
Are forever impressed on my mind—
Beautiful sunsets, spring weather
Friendly hollows with fallen leaves lined

The courage of first stars at evening
Bright sunshine and deep dark of night
Joy of meeting, reluctance at leaving
Moon's magic, mysterious light

Sheer delight at just being with you
Precious moments and dreams to share
Minutes and hours spent swiftly
Basking in love with you there.

The love that we've had is forever
Whatever the future may hold;
What you mean and always will mean to me
Will never grow faded or cold.

Just Five Years

I don't care about *forever*
Forever might be just a bit too long;
I pray just give us five good years together
The while our love continues true and strong.

We both know that life
Has its ups and downs
And we've listened to love's old sweet song;
Our memories will be
Sweeter for you and for me
'Cause we won't have to remember so long.

I don't care about *forever*
Forever might be just a bit too long;
I pray just give us five good years together
The while our love continues true and strong.

The Good Old Days

The good old days, the good old days
How well I remember the good old days
Like the week before last
When I held you so tight
The good old days
Like last Su-unday night.

The good old days, the good old days
Oh, how I long for the good old days
Like last week in the park
When the moon was so bright
The good old days
Like last Su-unday night.

I love the good ol' days when love was sweet, but then
All I've got to do is get together with you—love will repeat
  again.

The good old days, the good old days
Oh, how I love the good old days
Like the night before last
When our love was so right
The good old days
Like last Su-unday night.

So Beautiful

You make me feel so beautiful
You make me feel so beautiful
I need you to convince me that it's true
Because when you're not there to let me know you care
You leave me filled with doubt—alone and blue.

You make me feel so beautiful
You make me feel so beautiful
My mind keeps asking *Can it really be?*
But my heart believe it's so; when you hold me close, I know
The beauty of your wondrous love for me.

The mirror only makes me realize
It can't show me what's reflected in your eyes.

You make me feel so beautiful
You make me feel so beautiful
No one has ever loved me like you do
And your love makes me beautiful
Because I know I'm beautiful to you.

Your Nose Is Itchin'

[*Chorus*]
Your nose is itchin' and you're gonna kiss a fool
Ooh, ooh, ooh—I hope it's me
You're charmin' and bewitchin' and I'm gonna lose my cool
A kissin' fool is what I want to be.

An itchin' nose will never miss
It means someone will get a kiss
And it's supposed to be a fool;
Now it's finally come to pass
Your nose is itchin' awful fast
And I'm not gonna let you break that rule.

[*Repeat Chorus*]
If your nose itches now and then
I always want to be there when
That itchin', twitchin feel is takin' place
'Cause love is what it's leadin' to
And I'm the fool that's needin' you
It's plainer that the nose upon your face.

[*Repeat Chorus*]

Sweet Gift

Sweet gift that is mine
When you give me some time
An evening with you makes my dreams all come true
Nothing else is so fine
As when you give me some time.

Sweet gift that is mine
When you give me some time
A Sunday afternoon or a morning in June
Nothing else is so fine
As when you give me some time.

Sweet gift that is mine
When you give me some time
When you find yourself free, may it always be me
Nothing else is so fine
As when you give me some time.

Sweet gift that is mine
When you give me some time
It's your life that you share, and I know that you care for me
Nothing else is so fine
As when you give me some time
Sweet gift that is mine
When you give me some time . . .

I'm Gonna See My Baby

I'm gonna see my baby tonight
I'm gonna see my baby tonight
Though the day is just a-bornin'
I woke early in the mornin'
'Cause I'm gonna see my baby tonight.

There's gonna be a world of delight
When Baby smiles and whispers, "We might"
And the love that we will find
Will drive the shadows from my mind
I'm gonna see my baby tonight.

Waitin', waitin', waitin'
That's what I do worst
There'll be no celebratin'
While I'm anticipatin'
I need my arms around her first.

I'm gonna see my baby tonight
I know she'll be a beautiful sight
We'll have lovin' country style
All the stars are gonna smile
I'm gonna see my baby tonight
I'm gonna see my baby tonight
I'm gonna see my baby tonight.

I Want to Wake Up

When I'm weary and tired
And things have gone wrong
And I wish I were back on the farm
Then I don't give a "beep"
Where I lay down to sleep
But I want to wake up in your arms.

Anywhere sleep overtakes me
That's where I lay my head
I dream and I sleep like a baby
And pray you'll be there in my bed.

All the places I've been
All the places I've tried
I've found never a haven from harm
And I don't give a "beep"
Where I lay down to sleep
But I want to wake up in your arms
I don't give a "beep"
Where I lay down to sleep
But I want to wake up in your arms.

'Cause It's True

Never one to talk a lot
Least not while I'm with you
'Drather listen like as not
'N hold you till you're through
Then in the darkness
I'll whisper all my love for you.
Love you now and always will
I only sing it 'cause it's true.

I just listen all the while
I hold you to my breast
Loving every word and smile
As we do what we do best;
Then in the stillness
I'll whisper all my love for you
Love you now and always will
I only sing it 'cause it's true.

While we hold each other
I'll whisper all my love for you
Love you now and always will
I only sing it 'cause it's true.

Love Is for the Living

Love is for the living
Baby, this I know
Loving means forgiving
And Heaven here below;
All my life I've waited
For true love to arrive
Love is for the living
And, Baby, we're alive.

Trembling arms are waiting
For you to come inside
Our thoughts anticipating
A love that's so untried;
We may find love sweeter
Than honey from the hive
Love is for the living
And, Baby, we're alive.

Let's not waste a precious moment
Of our precious time;
Love is what life's all about
Without it, life ain't worth a dime.

Love that's true and tender
In our hearts will abide
Lips so soft and gentle
Will not be denied;
Doin' what comes naturally
Our love will grow and thrive
Love is for the living
And, Baby, we're alive
Love is for the living
And, Baby, we're alive.

Need You Near Me

Need you near me
Always near me
Baby, hear me
When I call
You're what I want for me
Don't ever set me free
—I want to fall.

But should you bid me go
I won't say no
To you it was always yes
Wouldn't try to phone
I'd cry alone
What I want most
—Is your happiness.

Need you near me
Ever near me
Baby, hear me
When I call
You're always on my mind
Without you I'll never find
No love at all
You're always on my mind
Without you I'll never find
No love at all, no love at all.

My Songs

The songs that I've done
Were for pleasure and fun
They were not for the world to hear
But each time I do one, when I have a new one
I want to sing it so sweet in your ear.

Now you say that my songs are all sounding the same
And I must admit that it's true
They never were written for fortune or fame
Every song that I wrote was for you
And because there is only one song in my heart
A song that says "Dear, I love you"
Every song that I sing, every bell that I ring
Keeps repeating "I love you, I love you"
Every musical note that I ever wrote
Sings "I love you, I love you, I love you."

Finders Keepers

It can happen in a church or in a diner
Or when you're standing on the corner of the street
You'll never know exactly where you'll find her
The one you've waited all your life to meet.

[*Chorus*]
Love, anytime, is beautiful
And the second time is more like a dream
I'll live the rest of my life
Wishing I'd known my wife
When we were both sixteen.

You may be twenty or a grandpa over sixty
Or a forty year old out to have some fun
But you'll know it when your heart starts doin' flipsies
That you've waited long enough—and she's the one.

[*Repeat chorus*]
So don't give up your searchin' and your hopin'
For a love that is tender and true
Then some special day a door will open
And the love you haven't found may find you.

[*Repeat chorus*]

Love Came Late

Love came late to you and me
Love came with maturity
We waited long and patiently.
Then love came late to you and me

Our mistakes are in the past
Our's is love that's bound to last
You mean everything to me.
Since love came late to you and me

We were destined for each other
Right from the start
You walked in and turned the key
That locked you in my heart.

Just in time you came to me
Youth is fine but as for me
I'm as happy as can be
That love came late to you and me.

I Need You

I need to kiss you
I need to kiss you
Need it more than I can say;
My lips remember
Your kisses tender
But they need to practice every day.

I need to hold you
Long to enfold you
I will shout it to the skies;
My arms must enfold you
And always hold you
Just because they need the exercise.

Your lilting, lovely laughter
Is the music I must hear;
I must see your smiling face
And know that you are near.

I need to love you
I want to love you
My lonely heart, without you, cries;
I long to love you
Must have your love true
Without your love something lovely dies.

What'll I Do?

I'm learning to live with loneliness
No stranger to sorrow and pain
But what'll I do with all this love
Until you're with me again?

I know how to smile through the tears
When the sun won't shine I choose rain
But what'll I do with all this love
Until you're with me again?

It won't turn off like a faucet or light
Can't hold it in, it's got me uptight;
By day I can't win, I'm a loser at night
And all because you've gone away, away, away, away . . .

You never will know how I miss you
Though you're gone all those memories remain
And what'll I do with all this love
Until you're with me again?

Christmas Lonely

The Christmas lights are all aglow
There's music in the air
We have our share of Christmas snow
Above the stars are everywhere
But Christmas isn't Christmas when a loved one's on the roam
It's Christmas down in Nashville
There's no Christmas here at home.

The shoppers hurry quickly by
Their minds on Christmas treats
With gifts and presents piled high
They pass on crowded streets
But Christmas isn't Christmas when a loved one's on the roam
It's Christmas down in Nashville
There's no Christmas here at home.

I hear the songs of Christmas
They're playing all the while
Though church bells chime their holy chimes
My smile's not a Christmas smile
'Cause Christmas isn't Christmas when a loved one's on the roam
It's Christmas down in Nashville
There's no Christmas here at home
It's Christmas all around the world
Still there's no Christmas here at home.

Whole Lot o' Woman

I don't go chasin' ponytails
Or gals I've never known
Don't look around for strayin' frails
Or widows all alone
They'll have to do without me
'Cause I know when I'm winnin'
I've got a whole lot o' woman
I don't need a whole lot o' women.

Let others try to play the field
And flit from here to there
My one-time lonely heart is healed
I'd trust it anywhere
I'm happy in her tender love
And I know when I'm winnin'
I've got a whole lot o' woman
I don't need a whole lot o' women.

Even when we're in a crowd
There's only her and me
I want to shout it right out loud,
"She's all the world to me."

My friends all know
Their wives are safe
I won't risk being burned
Those gals could be in outer space
As far as I'm concerned
I'll hold tight to the one I love
'Cause I know when I'm winnin'
I've got a whole lot o' woman
I don't need a whole lot o' women
Yeah! when you got a whole lot o' woman
You don't need a whole lot o' women!

Sorry

It hurts me when I hurt you, Baby
Makes me want to love you more
And I keep hopin' that maybe
You'll forgive me.

It hurts me so to see you cry
Can't bear to have you slam that door
And even though my eyes are dry
Tears of the soul flow.

Hurting you was farthest from my mind
Although I was a fool and I was blind

No need to say "I'm sorry, Baby"
My eyes reveal the hurt I bear
My ears are tuned to hear you say
"We may love and love again."

She'd Make a Bulldog Break His Chain

She looked so pert and pretty
When I saw her standing there
I liked her dress, her feminineness
And the way she did her hair
But when she turned and smiled at me
My heart got such a pain
I thought, *she's just the kind to make a bulldog break his chain.*

It was too much to expect that I could keep my self-control
Her every movement beckoned to my very heart and soul
The air was filled with music and I heard love's sweet refrain
And I thought, *she's just the kind to make a bulldog break his chain.*

If cake's not for the tasting, what's the good of all that icing?
If her love must go awasting
Why is she so enticing?
I tried to tell myself that she was far out of my class
But something else inside kept telling me to make a pass
I did—and now I'll never be that lonesome guy again
I know that she's the kind to make a bulldog break his chain.

Forgetting

I told myself when you went away
That after a short time, I'd be okay
That your memory would leave me
And then I'd be free
Oh! what a surprise for me.

I've tried food and liquor and wild, wild wimmin'
Religion, gambling, softball, and swimmin'
Swingin' and sominex, but still I find
That nothing ever takes you off my mind.

I told myself I'd have a helluva time
With all kinds of chances to dance and to dine
When I'd had all the worst
That remembering could give
I'd have a new chance to live.

But I've tried bowling, beer joints, and blind, blind dates
Lovin' in back seats and cuddlin' on skates
One-night stands but now I know I'll find
That nothing ever takes you off my mind.

I thought I could forget, but
It ain't never happened yet
'Cause your love is everlasting on my mind.

Moonlight Skate

The nights are long and lonely
And I never have a date
The weekend never seems to come
The days are running late
Then Saturday arrives and
It was surely worth the wait
Cause kissin' on the corners is really great.

I love to hold my baby
When I take her out to skate
And when she needs a partner
I'm there waitin' at the gate
Then I hug my honey dizzy
In a moonlight figure eight
And kissin' on the corners is really great.

And when we skate together
I know it won't be lonely like before
We could skate away forever
And when the music stops still ask for more, more, more.

There are other ways of lovin'
And a few to celebrate
I could take her to the movies
But I always hesitate
'Cause my lady is so lovely
And so loving when we skate
And kissin' on the corners is really great
Oh-oh, kissin' on the corners is really great!

I Lied

It wasn't the night that I told you I loved you
And called you the fairest of fair
Nor the time by the light of the moon up above you
When I whispered of how much I care
And it wasn't when we shared the dreams that could be
When I promised to ever be true
But the time that I told you
That I didn't love you
Was the last time I lied to you
That night when I told you that I didn't love you
Was the last time I lied to you.

Alone

I hear the music soft and sweet
It doesn't give me dancing feet
But, oh, it brings sweet memories
Like soft mist drifting on the breeze
And you return in dreams of bliss
Once more I know your tender kiss
The music of our own sweet song
Comes rushing on and lingers long
Sweet reveries of yesterday
Keep love alive—I wait and pray
You'll safe return.

You Stayed Away Too Long

You stayed away too long
And I've lost my song
Even the blues are gone
But I want you to know
That I still love you so
It's lonely but life goes on.
Yes, it's lonely, I still can't forget you
There's an ache where my heart has been
If only your sweet love would let you
Come back to my arms again.
You stayed away too long
And I've lost my song
Our parting won't lose its sting;
All I need is your love
And the heavens above
Will echo the love I sing
They will echo the love I sing.

Home with You

Whenever you're in my arms, I'm home
Whenever you're in my arms, I'm home
As long as you're there, our love to share
Whenever you're in my arms, I'm home.

Whenever you're in my thoughts, I dream
Whenever you're in my thoughts, I dream
Awake or asleep, those sweet memories I'll keep
Whenever you're in my thoughts, I dream.

Whenever our hearts are one, we love
Whenever our hearts are one, we love
Just being with you makes our love come true
Whenever our hearts are one, we love.

While You Were Away

I found myself singing the blues
I found myself singing the blues
I was sad and alone
With the bluest blues I've known
I found myself singing the blues.

Then I told myself, "Look here, you dum-dum
Where do you come off feeling sorry for yourself?
Nobody owes you anything.
If the books had to be balanced this very day
You've received and given more love
Than most people experience in two lifetimes.
So stop wallowing in the sorry self-pity
Of loneliness; turn to thoughts of joy
Such as memorable memories
The promise of pleasures to come
And count your blessings."
That's what I told myself
And that's what I tried to do
And do you know what?
Until your return, I still—

Found myself singing the blues
I found myself singing the blues
I was sad and alone
With the bluest blues I've known
I found myself singing the blues.

I'm Your Baby

The way you always know just what I'm needin'
And your love is there for everyone to see
You brightened up the dull life I was leadin'
I'm your baby, so come on and pamper me.

You're always thinking first of my desires
You make me feel I'm yours, and yet I'm free
You fan the flames of ever-youthful fires
I'm your baby, so come on and pamper me.

I never dreamed that any woman could be
All the woman that is you;
You make me think that an angel
Enjoys this heavenly feeling, too.

You gave your lovin' right from the beginnin'
More lovin' than I ever thought could be
And it never was so easy to be sinnin'
I'm your baby, so come on and pamper me.

Love

I've loved you in the starlight
And on sunny afternoons
I've loved you while the moon was shining bright
I've loved you to the music of a hundred different tunes
Or in stillness and it always seemed so right.

In daisy-sprinkled meadows
Or in green, pine-scented glade
We gave ourselves in love for love's own sake
No one can ever take the lovely memories we have made
While others slept, sweet love kept us awake.

Sweet love, oh yes
It all was ours
And evermore shall be
No one else can ever know
How sweet that love can be.

The world would not believe
Nor understand how much we care
That I could never ever leave
A place as long as you were there.

Sweet Licks

Not long ago a friend I know
Told me I had better go
She didn't want me any more.
I wanted love but she said, "Beat it!
You can't have your cake and eat it!"
I hollered back just as she slammed the door—

"I don't want to eat the cake
Or even know how much it's costing;
I don't want to eat the cake
I just want to lick the frosting!"

Now, here's a point I'd like to make.
The only way to have your cake
Is—eat it for internal pleasure
And have that memory to treasure
But as for me, this view I take—

"I don't want to eat the cake
Or even know how much it's costing;
I don't want to eat the cake
I just want to lick the frosting!"

Double Love

When we kiss and when we touch
I say, "I love you"
You say, "How much?"
Well, how much is "plenty"
Or what's "a great deal?"
It's hard to prove
How much love I feel.
But I want you to know that
My love has *clout*
And I'm using algebra
To work it out—
If y is you and x is me
Then z is love, undoubtedly
But the way the equation comes out true
Is x y = zz (double z)
That's double love for me and you.

Double love for you and me
Double love, Honey, can't you see
With all the love that's going round
Double love is what we've found.

Double love, we've got it good
Double love is our neighborhood
When not a single love is known
Double love will be our own.

Double love is where it's at
Double love has got us zapped
We can run but we can't hide
Double love is deep inside.

Double love is our delight
Double love's a shining light
Potluck may be others' lot
But double love is what we've got.

The Streak*

Back when I was just an itty-bitty kid
I always crept faster than the other babies did
And when I was doin' chores or playin' hide and seek
My mamma always said that I could—run like a streak.

Suddenly, now it's the latest style
To go streaking down the street wearing nothing but a smile
If you're not a sinner, you can be the first to speak
Life's a bare livin' when you—run like a streak.

I'll leave my clothes right here in the car
And I'll circle through the city, it won't be very far
Oh migosh, now, what a fix to be in
My clothes are in the car and I've—locked the key in.

So, go boy go, and run boy run
Be a-doin' of your thing and a havin' of your fun
Never mind the earth, just leave it to the meek
Outer space is yours when you—run like a streak
You can be in orbit when you—run like a streak
Life's a bare livin' when you—run like a streak.

*This is never going to compete with Ray Steven's great number "The Streak," but this was a brainchild before I heard his version of it; besides, why should he have all the fun?

Lonely but Hopeful*

"When you're away, I'm restless, lonely
Wretched, bored, dejected, only
Here's the rub, my darling dear
I feel the same when you are here!"*

Thus wrote one poet long ago
But then, of course, he couldn't know
The loneliness your absence brings
The blues my sad heart always sings
At parting—
But you'll come back, I'll wait till then
And love will rule our world again.

*By Samuel Hoffenstein.

The Lonesome Game

I think, *Forget-me-nots*
And I see eyes of blue
Petite forget-me-nots
Bring memories sweet of you
I see the wild geese fly
I breathe your name
And then I wonder why
Fools in love should try
The lonesome game.
I'm lonesome—oh, oh, so lonesome
The day you left was when the lonelies came
I'm lonesome—oh, oh, so lonesome
And now I know that no one ever wins
The lonesome game . . .

My Baby That Was

I'm leavin' my baby-that-was
She wasn't good to me
I'm leavin' that baby because
I wanna be with my baby-to-be.

They say that it's hard to be true
It never was hard for me
I never leave that baby-that-was
Till I find another baby-to-be.

I love them just one at a time
That's the way I was intended to be
You'll always find me walkin' the line
Till I find another baby-to-be.

So I'm leavin' that baby-that-was
She was drivin' me right out of my tree
I'm leavin' that baby-that-was
So I can be with my baby-to-be

My baby-that-was ain't my baby because
You see—
I wanna be with my baby-to-be.

Night Light (or Energy Crisis)

Now, I'm turning out my night-light
That pale little white light
I always left burning for you;
There's no hope anymore
That you'll darken my door
I know now we really are through.
Every time I'd see your smile
I'd keep hoping for a while
That you'd be coming back to me
But now I'm turning out my night-light
That pale little white light
'Cause I'm saving my energy.

I loved you through the darned ol' deep Depression
And I loved you all the way through World War Two
I loved you while the hippies' self-expression
Was the thing that everyone was supposed to do;
I thought our love was solid as a rock
Until the day you said it was a crock—
Still, I kept hoping . . .

But now I'm turning out my night-light
That pale little white light
I always left burning for you;
There's no hope anymore
That you'll darken my door
I know now we really are through.
Everytime I'd see your smile
I'd keep hoping for a while
That you'd be coming back to me
But now I'm turning out my night-light
That pale little white light
'Cause I'm saving my energy.

Just a Common Pup

I'm just a common pup
No need to brag me up
Though my slavey's got
A college degree;
Still, he never bites
Or violates my rights
He always takes good care of me.

I'm just a common pup
My food I lap it up
Or sometimes I just wolf it down
But either way, it makes the neighbors say
I'm the most productive dog in town.

A dog's life is not very hard
As long as I can "go"
In my neighbor's yard—

I water common trees
And harbor common fleas
Bite the mailman
In a common place
I leave my common hair
Almost everywhere—
My odor is a common disgrace.

I'm just a common pup
No need to brag me up
Though my slavey's got
A college degree;
Still, he never bites
Or violates my rights
He always takes good care of me.

Queen Loretta

She's the queen of country music
She has reigned for oh, so long
She'll be our queen of country music
As long as there's a song.

And our queen of country music
Is so wonderf'ly sincere
Her presence brings us happiness
Each time she does appear.

She never hoards the charm she has to share;
Her voice comes like an angel's through the air.

Our queen of country music
Deprive us of her never
Our own sweet Queen Loretta
Please let her reign forever.

Empty Cookie Jar*

My mama taught me early
As she said, "Now listen, girly
And I'll teach you all the things you need to know.

To keep a fella happy
Just like your dear ol' pappy
Remember that you reap just what you sow.
Make love an everyday thing
And when he wants a plaything
Don't let him leave home wishin' on a star
Bake lots of cookies in the oven
'Cause there's nothin' cools the lovin'
Any quicker than an empty cookie jar.

'Cause a man that gets his cookies right at home
Will have everything he needs and never roam.

Make him want to lay his head
On the pillow in your bed
If the love he needs is there, he won't stray far
Fill his nights with memories
Make his dreams realities
And never have an empty cookie jar."
Don't you ever have an empty cookie jar
—That's what Mama told me.

*This song was written for a female vocalist and as soon as I find the right girl—I'm going to make her a STAR!

Summer's Gone

Summer's gone
And still your memory
Lingers in my mind
Like sweet perfume.

While I dream
My lonely reverie
Paints your lovely face
Across the room.

Blustery winds of autumn
Sing their songs, reminding me
Summer love once ended
Nevermore shall be.

Our paths have parted
And more apart go on;
Our love was born in summer
And summer's gone—

Crumhorn Summer's Gone*

Summer's gone
Yet Crumhorn's memories
Go misting through my mind
Dispelling gloom

While I dream
My lonely reverie
Brings smiling Crumhorn faces
To my room

Blustery winds of autumn
Sing their songs, reminding me
Crumhorn days in memory
Remain eternally—

Crumhorn dreams
Will stay with us forever;
Those joys will leave us never
Though summer's gone.

*A longtime love affair with a superb summer Boy Scout camp can create some super memories (alternate lyrics to "Summer's Gone").

———*

As I was walking down the street
A billboard met my eye
The advertisements written there
Would make you laugh and cry
The wind and rain came down that night
Washed half that board away
The other half remaining there
Would make that billboard say—

Oh, smoke a Coca Cola
Tomato catsup cigarettes
See Lillian Russell wrestle
With a box of Oysterettes
Heinz's pork and beans
Will meet again
For the finish fight
And Silent Joe
Will speak about
Sopolia tonight—

Get Purina for the horses
It is the best in town
Castoria kills the measles
Just pay five dollars down
Teeth are removed without a pain
Costs but half a dime
And overcoats are selling out
A little at a time.

*A song remembered from early youth (I still recall the melody also but neither the source nor author).

My Modern Verse

Cast a vote for constipation
Hurry down to the last drop
Fly the friendly preparation
It's H when you can't plop
Cross your heart and don't leave home
If stranded on an isle
We Chevrolet the old-fashioned way
In Pepto-Levi style

Let your fingers leave the driving
Maxwell House to spell relief
The National Bank & Trust to luck
Will help you drown your grief
Invest your funds at Barney's Bar
The interest there is high
Your auto will go long and far
With brakes from Walt & Vi.

Gordy's Song*

When I was young and devil-may-care
I told a lady, young and fair,
"Although I'm sowing my wild oats
If you'd love me, then—*love my goats.*"

She declined, but in my mind
I still had hopes that I might find
A gal whose perspicacity
Would let her love both goats *and* me.

Now I'm sort of settled down
On this little farm outside of town,
"Kathy, Honey, look and see
Who I've brought for company."

She's the gal that changed my life
She's the one I made my wife;
Our life is perfect harmony
She loves my goats and also *me.*

My bachelor days were scarcely missed
(A goat's not much for bein' kissed)
Now, though there's silver in our hair
Those goats and love are always there.

---

*Gordy was a friend who was deeply committed to improving the image of the dairy goat and to publicizing it's value to humanity. In appreciation of Gordy's efforts, I wrote this song. My brother, Bob, and I sang it at the National Dairy Goat Convention at Ithaca, New York, in 1974.

Together we would tend our goats
And in-between we'd sow wild oats
Now, I suppose it's time to stop
But we sure raised a bumper crop.

Five hundred kids and four strong sons
Ain't we been the lucky ones?
Though we're married, we feel free
Those goats are common property.

We had to buy a larger plot
Those goats sure kid around a lot;
Sometimes one or two or three
We milked them to prosperity.

Thus ends this song of love and goats
And, don't forget, those *wild, wild oats;*
The smartest words I ever wrote
Were: "If you'd love me, then—*love my goats."*

Part IX

Travel

Unlike today's generation, we believed that a lifetime of work and service were required as a prelude to (hopefully) leisure and travel. Hence, as a self-designated "homebody," this is not—and rightfully so—a major category.

My Little Map Reader and Me

We're on a trip and as I drive
My wife plays a vital part;
She reads the map, watches the signs
And each day's course does chart.

Life's road is very like that, too.
We're headed for, I don't know
She checks the map and plots the course
—And tells me where to go!

Broad-minded

The highway sign reads USE TWO LANES
That shook me for a minute
There's only one lane I can use
And I'm already in it.
Yet I don't want to violate
The highway rules of the Empire State
However absurd or bizarre
And so, to comply, I must go out and buy
A bigger and much wider car.

Grand Canyon

Ah yes, 'tis truly GRAND
A masterpiece in a special world
All its own. It's more than rock and sand
Unique in all its special beauty
Created not by human hands
But by the Maker, with His special tools—
The wind, the snow and ice, the rain.
This massive wonderland endures
Resists erosion's stress and strain
Defies the passing eons
And just by being GRAND
Belittles the accomplishments
Of unmighty, mortal man.
While man, in turn, reviews
In awe, his humility restored
As he, enraptured, gazes at
The monumental sculpture of the Lord.

Ocean Lover's Observation

There are never enough of oceans
Wind and wave never cease to enthrall;
Let it never be said that like bosoms
"When you've seen two—you've seen them all."

New Mexico

In six days did God make the earth
That's what the preacher postulates
For whatever *that* is worth.
The scientist, in turn, declares
That it's round instead of flat.
My question, "Lord, New Mexico
Did you make it just like that
On purpose?" My candid observation
While simply passing through it,
"If God *did* make New Mexico
—The devil made him do it."

PS: Discriminatory? Perhaps, but then
I thought that very thing again
Of Nevada, Utah, and Arizona.

Haiti

The hazy hills of Haiti
Rising bleakly from the sea
Bespeak the sad condition
Of a poor economy.

Where agriculture fails to flourish
History teaches is despair
Poverty is rampart
Prosperity is rare.

One can't raise corn and taters
On lava rock and sand
And land not fit for tillagae
Indeed, is barren land.

Dependable Dawn

In the sunrise do I put my trust
I know that it will be
The dawn will dispel the darkness
Whether on land or sea.

Obscured by clouds or blazing forth
It surely will be there
All a part of God's wonderful plan
The light of the world to share.

How fortunate that the Almighty
Still holds in his orderly hand
Sun, earth, moon, and stars, the cosmos
All, eternally at His Command.

Imagine what dire disaster
What chaos soon would loom large
Should He reliquish His constant control
And let governments be in charge.

Solitary Whale

In the last rays of the setting sun
We saw a whale
Well, half of one
He only showed his tail
And then as if to emphasize
The sad plight of his species
He pointed tail up to the skies
Without a query or a cry
He gently waved good-bye.

Queen Elizabeth II Crisis

The great ship lost all power
And wallowed aimlessly
Between the troughs and billows
At the mercy of the sea.

Although highly inconvenient
We could stand the stress and strain
Just so glad we're on a vessel
Instead of—on a plane.

A Thank You
(To the Golden Spa Health Club personnel aboard the QE II in '85.)

To the golden girls
Of the Golden Spa
Who open the golden door
To vim and vigor and better health
We'll be grateful forevermore.

They go out on a limb
To make us feel trim
They exhort us to efforts severe;
When we get home, they expect us
To continue as if we were here.

From their charms we may never recover
In our hearts each one of us knows
When they cast their sweet spell
They could easily sell—
Freezers to Eskimos.

Oceans

The world keeps turning round, of course
Not much excitement there
And outer space is nothing much
Just out there in the air
But for sheer mystery and commotion
Ever awesome, changing, free
There's no wonder like the ocean
God's restless, perpetual motion sea.

Caribbean Clouds

Billowing clouds in the distance
Join the sea to the sky
They seem to have no other function
Than just to keep passing by
Still, the shapes they assume are of beauty
And I have a powerful notion
Theirs is a compelling duty
To enhance and embellish the ocean.

A Memory of Cape Cod

Squealing and wheeling
They wing o'er the waves
Sea birds whirling in graceful flight
Dipping and diving
Ever in motion
Throughout every day
Only resting by night.
Family are they—
For every father there is a mother;
One good tern deserves another.

Maine—First Impressions

Maine will long endure
Though popple, pine, and hemlock
The view somewhat obscure;
The foundation is of solid rock
Its people, tough as leather
Withstand the seasonal tourist shock
And winter's vilest weather
In this land of small, dark streams
And bright, old-fashioned dreams.

Senior Hot Rods

When we're traveling far
And going by car
We get on the interstate.
No thirty-mile zones or stop lights
Our speed is a gamble with fate.
We're heading for places
A long way away
If we don't have a flat or a stall
The way that we're hell-bent
We'll get there today—
Or we may not get there at all.

There's a car on the side
With the hood open wide
It's steaming, as hot engines will;
Rolling at sixty, we pass on by
—As if *it* were standing still.

Close Encounter

Speed Limit Strictly Enforced
Reads the message stern;
Everyone's doing the limit and more
As the wheels continue to churn.

Speed Enforced by Radar is
The next sign that I'm reading
But Radar is busy filming for "MASH"
We all keep right on speeding.

Speed Patrolled by Aircraft
I look up and I see a crow.
Crows and I are on real good terms
So we speed on, flying low.

Around a curve and over a knoll
A police car we suddenly see;
His flasher is on, he's turning around
And he's looking right at me.

I'm holding my breath and saying a prayer
And hoping I'm still not dead
Just cruising along at fifty-five
With that halo above my head.

Halifax
(Nova Scotia)

Where earth and sea and sky
Are mingled neatly
Trees cast their shade.
Where forever, now, and history
Join discreetly—
A city modern, rooted in the past.

Despite severe nomadic leanings
That create an urge to roam
In my heart I know for certain
That were Halifax *my* home—
I'd make tracks
To Halifax.

Millie's Micmacs*
(Our tour guide.)

Millie's Micmacs went to Halifax
They were bright and cheerful;
When Millie told them what was what
—They really got an earful.

[*Chorus*]
Millie's Micmacs are a tribe
Defying all description;
They're afflicted by the curse
Of traveling's addiction.

*To the tune of "Yankee Doodle."

Tour

Now we board our faithful bus
We hope that it will carry us
From here to there and home again
No wear and tear, no sweat nor strain.

Nova Scotia Tour

On Friday morning early
Our bus was feeling tourly
So we headed out with everyone aboard
Across New York and Mass.
We swiftly then did pass
Though we gave them all the time we could afford.

Then we headed north to Maine
—Sometimes in the rain—
Mainly because Maine was on our way.
We crossed the Bay of Fundy
The next day, which was Sunday
And had two days in Halifax to play.

As we took the Cabot Trail
Lofty mountains we did scale
The while we viewed majestic scenery.
Then we sailed to P.E.I.
Where the farms are neat as pie
And we eyed the agricultural greenery.

Across we sailed once more
To that North New Brunswick shore
Soon to that imaginary line
To the good old U.S.A.;
Now it's homeward all the way
To New York, a state that suits us mighty fine.

Now that we'll soon be home
I will end this epic poem
With, "We give our thanks to Millie and to Jack;
We were happy on that day
When they took us on our way
And we thank the Lord they brought us safely back."

Cabot's Trail
(N.S. tour '86.)

We climbed the Cabot Trail
And like a ship without a sail
It really had us going roun' and roun';
The ascent was pretty steep
As we slowly up did creep
And we crawled a snaily pace while comin' down.

The scenery was just *grand,*
And the trip, so nicely planned
Included food and sunshine for the day;
We'll remember well the time
That we spent on Cabot's climb
For we thoroughly enjoyed it all the way.

Where the Heart Is

I went where highways led me
Where'er wheels and motor sped me
Urban sights or country grandeur
No strangers were to me.
We saw relatives and friends
Learned the highway never ends
—But continues on
From sea to shining sea.

We saw buildings big and smaller
Some skyscrapers were taller
Small towns flew by—
We viewed the Capitol's dome.
We've reached the realization
Our most important destination
From anyplace at all is
"Home, sweet home."

Home Again

Homeward bound.
How sweet the sound
After days of travel over land and sea;
Some folks may like to roam
But just the thought of *home*
Sends a special feeling stealing over me.
So let the nomads wander
To foreign climes "out yonder"
Explore exotic ruin, view majestic dome
While they trod the shifting sands
Fulfillment seek in other lands
I'll be happy and contented here at *home*.

Virginia Tour

Memories pleasant will long endure
Of our historic Virginia tour
Where in hall and tavern
In church and manse
Our men of courage
Once took a chance
Staking their lives on liberty
With deeds that set our nation free.
We walked where those stalwarts once did trod
And sensed that *their* course was ordained by God.

Easy Does It
(*Bus tour*)

If you're planning to go away from home
Your itchy feet have the urge to roam
Don't throw your belongings into the trunk
Pile into your car and take off like a drunk;
Let the "Pathfinder" find the way for you
Then enjoy and be carefree is all you do.
If you're heading to Salem or Norfolk and back
Leave the planning to Doris—the driving to Jack.

Williamsburg, Virginia

Old Williamsburg is staid and stern
And judging by anything we can learn
They say it hasn't changed at all
Since patriots answered freedom's call.

We checked the taverns and trod the streets
That rang to fife and bugle's beats.
Why Patrick, George, and Tom, and Will
Have ALL slept here—and drunk their fill.

It seems that time has here stood still
That every art and craft and skill
Has been preserved as in days of yore
And, thus, will remain for evermore.

From the time the pilgrims touched our land
The entire order was devised and planned
All of history was divined and made—
With an eye toward exploiting tourist trade.

McAdoo, Pennsylvania

Do residents of Mcadoo
Doo all the things that others doo?
And when all is Mcadid and done
—Do they Mcaddiddle just for fun?

Claudia and Jackie
(Tour guides par excellence.)

In both '87 and '88
Two tour guides worked
Both early and late
Lending both charm and expertise
So a bus load of tourists would be at ease.

Claudia and Jackie, please be aware
We've appreciated your loving care;
We'd recommend you, without reservation
To any travelers on vacation.

Our thanks for your efforts on our behalf
For the times that you made us smile or laugh;
You'll remain in our hearts—
Though we're far away
When we think of you
It will brighten our day.

Part X

Economics—Politics—Taxes

And a brief reminiscence of thirty-five years of postal employment.

Part X
Taxpayers Leaned on Taxing Up to Death

Economics—Politics—Taxes

Taxpayer's Lament or Taxing Us to Death

I worked hard for many a day
And when I drew my pay
I thought, of course, the money would be mine
But *they* kept part of my dough
To pay tax for earning it, and so—
I just took the rest and mumbled, "Fine."
Meanwhile, the part I kept
Had dwindled while I slept.
They said, "Inflation really is a bandit."
Then when I paid my bills
To add to all my ills
Once again they taxed me just to spend it.

Oh, they tax us when we earn it
And they tax us if we burn it
They tax us if we squander or we save
They tax us if we lend it
And they tax us when we spend it
Even when we spend it for our grave.
They tax us when we eat
And they tax us while we sleep
They tax us if we work or if we play
If we stay home sick in bed
Or if we take a trip instead
They tax us every step along the way.

If we send the kids to college
They tax us for the knowledge
If we marry then they tax us for our bliss
But if we stay in single state
They tax us at a higher rate
To be certain that we pay for every kiss.

So we'll pay and pay and pay
They'll get our money anyway
But we'll kick until we hear the final bell.
If we should go to where the greeter
Should chance to be the good Saint Peter
The tax on the admission will be Hell.
They say, "Can't take it with you"
Here's a real good reason why
They'll have it all before the final show.
We didn't have it when we came
And we'll leave here just the same;
Taxes took it—WHAT A WAY TO GO!

"Fixed" Income

I hear of people on "fixed" income.
Well, it seems to me everyone's on a "fixed" income.
They've fixed it so the taxes take most of it.
They've fixed it so there's not enough to pay the bills.
They've fixed it so there's not enough to go around.
They've fixed it so the income doesn't equal the outgo.
Fixed income has got us all in a fix.

Political Poverty

> NEWS ITEM(S): *Jesse Jackson spent the night with a poor family in Harlem, Brooklyn, Binghamton, et cetera, et cetera, et cetera, ad infinitum.*

All my life, I practiced
Just trying to be "pore"
Ready for the big campaign
Of nineteen eighty-four
But the primaries are over
And in spite of life austere
My home feels sad neglected
'Cause Jesse never slept here.

In spite of all my efforts
At embracing poverty
(Even tried to get on welfare
Back in nineteen eighty-three)
No one rang my doorbell
And I must survive the shame
We're just as "pore" as anyone
—But Jesse never came.

May as well burn my credentials
And accept my "pore" position
I know I'll never be a part
Of someone's rainbow coalition
So my smile has turned to frowning
My eye has shed a tear
We're just as "pore" as anyone
—But Jesse never slept here.

Un-Success Story

I had this little business
Called it Urban Sanitation.
It was like a thousand others
That thrive throughout our nation.

I was feeling properous
And some folks even say
That I was doing well indeed
While cleaning up each day.

But the city got into the act
With trucks and men they started
To haul away the refuse
That I had always carted.

So folks no longer needed
The service I had offered
Their taxes paid to haul away
The garbage I once chauffered.

Now I'm unemployed and broke
My back is to the wall
But more than that—I'm living proof
You can't fight City Haul!

Unemployed

"The economy's improving;
In fact, it's going great."
So the president to the nation
Emphatically did state
But *I* haven't had a paycheck
For weeks and months on end.
My patience and my credit
Have gone past the power to bend.
"Unemployment is receding
And production's on the rise."
That doesn't hide the dull despair
In a hungry family's eyes
'Cause the plant will not reopen
In Pittsburgh or in Dayton
And our bills are piling up
While we're job hunting and waitin'.
I still want to feed my family
We don't ask for charity
Lord, just give us a depression
—Can't *stand* this *prosperity.*

S O B*
(Save our bridge.)

The man stood on the battered bridge
And cried out, "All is lost."
That bridge had served with honor
As off to school he'd crossed
And to get to Sunday ballgames
Or to take his wife, in labor—
To fight the blazing fire
In the homestead of his neighbor.

But the town board has decided
That we couldn't stand the cost
Of repairs and renovations—so
In the trash can would be tossed
Our faithful bridge, and loyal
That stood by us throughout time
But to some who still remember
This would seem to be a crime.

Perhaps, like brave Horatius
With fearful sword in hand
Upon that doomed and dismal span
We all should make a stand
Or if our own Lady Godiva
Would go riding through our town
Maybe *she'd* convince the board
Not to burn our bridges down.

*The local town board voted to demolish a bridge rather than rebuild it.

First-Class Male

I got oodles of mail, yes, I did
The kind advertisers all send
And my bills promptly came
Addressed to my name
But—no letter from a friend.

So this week that was born full of hope
Came to a discouraging end
My check didn't come
But that was ho hum
To—no letter from a friend.

I worked extra hours and fiercely
So the woebegone days I could spend;
Here's mail from the truck
But I'm out o'luck
'Cause—no letter from a friend.

Now, I don't know much 'bout Heaven
Heard more of that other place
But whatever my lot, like it or not
I can stand the fall from grace
I can bear whatever I have to
I can weather the warming trend
But where'er I may be
Just don't deprive me
Of my letters from a friend
(You could write them on asbestos).

To All Postal Employees

Some draw funny pictures
And some make silly jokes;
It's the fashion nowadays
To ridicule the postal folks.

But the service doesn't falter
No matter what *they* say;
Hard working postal people
Bring mail to us every day.

So when Christmas bells are ringing
And we're blest with Christmas cheer
We'll give thanks as we remember
Joys you bring through all the year.

Please Write

I like your letters, short or long
We'll leave that up to you;
I make my pitch and hope your pen
Will bat a letter back again.
Each letter from a friend, it's true
Increases postal revenue.

Super's Shorthanded Lament

As I early go to my daily tasks
I wonder along the way
Will there be persons enough to get the job done
Or will there be the devil to pay?
Will I have enough help to distribute the mail
And to man every route and jeep?
How many people will call in "sick"?
How many will oversleep?

I had a dream that I died last night
And I went right straight to Hell;
The devil met me at the gate
And I said, "Sir, can you tell me
If we've got enough help to do the job right?"
With a devilish grin, as he let me in, he said,
"Hell, no! I thought you knew—
We *always* work with a skeleton crew!"

The Day Before Christmas
(Apologies to Clement Clarke Moore.)

'Twas the day before Christmas
The mail was all sent
Some arrived broken and some arrived bent.
The letters were left by the carriers with care
At places where people were no longer there.
The postmaster sipped his coffee downtown
Then hurried back to turn the radio down.
The clerks were there, yawning;
Those who were awake
Threw a whole tray of mail
Before taking a break.
A rural carrier, back in his cage
Pondered his pipe between moments of rage
And vowed that he'd sit right there on his tail
Till his helper came in to deliver the mail.
One lonesome window clerk lit up a smoke
To him the whole operation was just a big joke.
Meanwhile the super was pulling his hair
And wracking his brain
(He didn't have much to spare)
BUT THE MAIL WAS DELIVERED
Before it came night—
MERRY CHRISTMAS, YOU GUYS
You put up a good fight!

Postal Retirement

It's not "just a job" that they're leaving, you see
It's a plus thirty years of reliability.
It's devotion to duty and doing one's best;
It's working the tough days along with the rest.
How many the parcels, whoever can say?
Or the myraids of letters taken care of each day?
They've accepted and canceled and sorted these years
They've dispatched and delivered along with their peers.
And now that they're leaving the chaos and strife
What they really are leaving, is a way of life.
And still it's not over—that's not where it ends
Those duties they'll leave in the hands of good friends.
Good post office friends, who never will fail
To remember
When Ed, Jack, and Harry were *moving* the mail.

Part XI

Potpourri

A catchall of the many and varied subjects that have fallen prey to an indiscriminate pen.

Food for Thought

Nutritionists are wont to say
That we *are* what we eat;
Methinks, sir, you must masticate
—A lot of donkey meat!!

The Bright Side

When things have gone wrong
In your life, there's no song;
You feel you can't go on any longer.
Get your mind off your sorrow
'Cause there's always tomorrow
—And things *could* go a lot *wronger!*

Color Preference

May my thumb be green and my eyes be blue
May my teeth be as white as snow
May my hair be silver, my skin be tanned
And brushed by soft breezes that blow.
Don't let my thoughts be sullen or dark
But sunny and golden instead, and
While we're verbally splashing the colors around
—Let my blood and my poems be read.

Unbreakable

It's best, when falling, Lady fair
To fall upon the derriere
'Cause it won't break or even bend
But it sure gets you in the end.

Technology *Is* Wonderful

We are very scientific
As to medical concerns;
We understand the universe
And the way it spins and turns.

Aerodynamics help us fly
Robots built our car
Computerized technology
They say will take us far.

We make clones and test-tube babies
Synthetic cloth and leather
And then we get our woodchuck out
To predict six weeks of weather.

Rubik's Cube

I don't have to
Yet I must.
Some dictatorial directive
In my mind forces me
To twist and turn
Rotate and gyrate
Knowing I can't win
Or draw or make a gain.

Perhaps, if I can wear it out
Then as it falls upon the floor
In twenty-seven tiny blocks
I'll sweep it up and with a smile
Deposit in a circular file.

With My Bare Face Hanging Out

I saw the sign upon the door
But still I ventured in
Hoping no one in the store
On me the crime would pin.
NO BARE FEET the sign did read
Will anybody heed?
No one will ever realize
I'll be just ever so discreet
That in this pair of socks and shoes
Are a pair of bare, bare feet.

Listen—Ye Shall Hear

Listen to your body
That's what the experts say
Listen to your body
When you exercise or play.
Listen to your body
When *it* feels pain or hurt
—I listened to *my* body
And all it said was
"Pr-r-r-r-r-r-r-t."

Woods Lover

I may be the forests' prime evil
I'm at home with the hemlock and pine
Sassafras and sycamore are both good friends of mine
In hickory, oak, or beech, I'm a wily woodland elf
I just hope that I'm not lost in the woods
—and making an ash of myself.

Addicted

My car is hooked on gas
It just won't run on water
It won't go at all
On alcohol
Been that way since I bought her.

It takes twenty gallons of Arab juice
To fill the tank to the spout
It won't even try
If the tank goes dry
The motor just sputters out.

I weaned it off "cold turkey"
And gave it nothing but spark
But without any gas
Alack and alas
All it would do was *park*.

So I tolerate its bad habit
And don't let it know how it hurts
To be spending my cash
For that devilish gas
That it piddles away in spurts.

Financial Propanity

The various bills arrive regularly
Sure as taxes and death and the rain;
However obscene the others may be
We speak of fuel bills in language propane.

You Over There

Over there you have the "old" world
While here we have the "new"
You old-world folks think it's a plus
That you contributed to us;
You sent your "tired, hungry, poor"
To populate our "shore to shore."
Lest you become smug and content
Here's a list of things you also sent:

The German measles and Asian flu
Dutch elm disease, to name a few;
English sparrows, Norwegian rats
Japanese beetles, and Siamese cats;
Russian vodka, a genuine curse
(It competes with the booze that we make worse);
The Mafia, Italy's favorite sons
We've had better heritage straight from the slums;

Cocaine you send from everywhere
Along with lice, you gladly share;
And then there's terrorists and spies
Propaganda, and bold-faced lies.
There's a whole lot more, but that's enough
So you know we could do without that stuff;
We plead—don't send us any more
Of your pests, diseases, and "old-world" wars.

Who *Mis*names These Things?

I went to a "flea market" just to see
What foolish mortals would pay a fee
To own a flea.
Then on to the "pool hall," intending to swim;
One look at my swimsuit, they jeered,
"Look at him."
I dashed in the "rest room," quick as a flash
Hoping to get a nap, but alas
There was no place to sleep
Or even fall in a heap
—Only water-filled traps.
I thought in a "pantry" I'd surely find pants
Yet nary a pair did I find.
Called the "Fire Department" to light up my fire;
They told me, "You're out of your mind."
Now to point out a *major* misnomer
One that left me especially wroth
I entered a bustling "brothel"
Expecting a bowl of broth.

Language Barrier

The peculiarities of our language
Are hard to understand
Why do we say "man-eating tiger"
When it's a tiger-eating man?

Must It *b*?

It's hard to understand why somb
Words end with *b*, for instance, thumb.
When we add two numbers, do we get a sumb?

I've sometimes gone way out on a limb
And just because of a personal whimb
Our towels are embossed with HER and HIMB.

When I groom my hair I use a comb
Do as the Romans when I'm in Romb
At the end of the day I hurry homb.

Whenever I find myself in a jamb
I claim to be "innocent as a lamb"
Otherwise I'm a close-mouthed clamb.

To arrive at the top of a hill we climb
A bell in the steeple peals out a chimb
While my verse has oft been known to rhymb.

If it's level or straight we say it's plumb
But a crummy *b* on words like crumb
Seems to me to *b* pretty damb dumb.

Sure Thing

"She can put her shoes under my bed anytime."
That's a fact of which there's no doubt
And if she pounds on my door
At a quarter past four
I'm not gonna let her *out*!!

Play on Words

This language is confusing
Sometimes it's most amusing
With meanings that are various and strange
A *lemon* is an auto or a fruit;
Threads are on a bolt, but also it's a suit
And a pasture or a stove is called a *range*.

Those words with meanings double
Give us lots and lots of trouble
Since they seem to mean so many different things.
Does *cheesecake* always mean a "dish"?
A *dream* is a girl, a sleep, a wish
And ringing bells and dolts are *ding-a-lings*
—Also, certain poets.

Of Animal (and Human) Behavior

A lion will roar
When he's hungry or sore;
A mouse will squeak from fear;
A bull will bellow
So glad he's a fellow
And happy that he's not a steer;
A cow will moo
Just for something to do;
Just for fun, a jackass will bray;
It's a well-known fackle
That a hen will cackle
Without even intending to lay.

Permanent?

To the beauty parlor a wife must go
Eager to spend thirty bucks or so
To get her hair "done"—when the money is spent
She has what they call a "permanent."
The incongruous fact, of which nobody speaks
Is—a "permanent" only lasts two weeks.

Meanwhile
The husband avoids the barbershop
(He doesn't have *anything* left on top);
The hair that in youth was so glossy and black
Is gone forever—it won't come back.
His cute, curly locks have long since went
I'd say he's the one with the "permanent."

Waiter?

Another example of misused words
Which upon my nerves has been grating;
We call the server a "waiter," but
It's the *diner* who does all the waiting.

Compatible

We're *not* a "tacky" couple
In spite of all that's been said;
My wife never comes to the point
—And *I* can't get a head.

In Defense of Small Strawberries

Don't say that berry's too small
To provide us with strawberry flavor
He is willing to give his all
Making our taste buds quaver.

Whence came that colossal right
To discard at very first sight?
Did Jesus scorn the widow's mite?
Or spurn the candle's puny light?

Because something or someone is little
Doesn't mean he's a cull or an elf;
You see, I'm sort of caught in the middle
—I once was little myself.

Phony Greeter

I think that I have never viewed
Acquaintance quite so crass and crude
As one who greets with "How are you?"
Then rushes on nor slackens pace
Without a pause or moment's grace
To let me say a word or two
About the way I feel or am.
His actions show his words are sham
—He really doesn't give a damn.

A Day That Will Live?

The ides of March made infamous
In days of Julius Caesar
Is ominous cause Brutus chose
To murder that old geezer.

And April first has ever been
At home, at work, in schools
A special day for humans
—A holiday for fools.

Now, March the thirty-first bids fair
In history's solemn tome
To steal the scene, the spotlight's glare
—Should God take Oral *home*.

Soul-Searching Study

An out-of-the-body experience
It seems that some can achieve
While we who are so attached to ourselves
Are much more reluctant to leave.

I'd like to be able to add "me, too"
To accounts of taking an impersonal view
Of the personal body down below
While my spirit was bathed in a heavenly glow

But in all my hours, awake or in slumber
Not one out-of-the-body journey I find
Though I can recall times without number
When I was told, "You're out of your mind!!"

Early Lesson

Of the tree of knowledge of good and evil
Adam and Eve did eat
So they were expelled from paradise
Tossed out in the street.
What was the knowledge Adam gained
To compense for such sacrifice?
He learned that those of the opposite sex
Are not perfect—though ever so nice.

Rheum for Improvement

I won't deny that a tasty dish
Can cause my mouth to water
An icy wind will make my nose
Run much more than it oughter

But if I must have moisture seeping
And creeping, like morning dew
Then let it be from my tear-filled eyes
—I'll have a rheum with a view.

Age-old Question

At forty-five I married
But she was just fifteen
So I was three times older
That's easy to be seen.

But should I live to sixty
Then she would thirty be
And I'd be only *twice* as old
Do you think she'll out-age me?

Perfect Gift

It seems appropriate to give
Something of beauty to one who is beautiful
Something intellectual to one who is
Intelligent, wise, and dutiful.
There is always a "perfect" gift one can send
To any imperfect acquaintance or friend
But matching a suitable gift to a givee
Is an art full of ifs, ands, and buts
And I wonder why is it friends give me
So frequently—gifts of nuts?

[*Addendum*]
My sister sends "light verse"
I like it better than the dark kind;
Rhymed humor makes the gloom disperse
And never overloads my mind.

Electric Eel

An eel sat sobbing on the floor
Of ocean's briny deep;
I snorkeled by a time or four
And asked, "Why do you weep?"

"I've lost my husband," she replied
"He'd high voltage in his day
Till his generator shorted out
And then he passed away."

"Do you miss him awfully much
Strong love for him still feel?"
"He lit my light, he turned me on
—I miss him a good eel."

Choir Director
(To Bob, in appreciation.)

He coaxes, cajoles, and bullies the choir
Hoping to somehow infuse or inspire
Exalt and exhort them to heights unattained
—Excellence seeking where mediocrity reigned.
Though perfection will never be reached, on the whole
Perfection is always his ultimate goal.
And the director's reward for his trouble and care?
More furrowed his brow, less numbers his hair
But his ear catches strains that bring fond memories
Of when voices were blended in sweet harmonies.

Synonym

Doing the crosswords has made me refined
By putting a host of new words in my mind.
For instance, I no longer blurt the word "ass"
When conversing with someone stupid and crass
Now I label him *onager* and more likely than not
He thinks a compliment he himself has just got;
I'm just as content with the point that I've made.
By any other name—a *spade* is a spade.

Grand Larceny?

"It is a sin to steal a pin;
It is a sin to steal a rotten tater."
That's what my mother taught me;
It stood me in good stead later.

A thought, while I pensively pause to peruse
What the lawyers and judges have planned;
My mother would never have been convinced
That *any* kind of larceny is *grand*.

A Modern Youth

His feet are firmly on the ground
(Well, one is on the throttle)
His hands are on the wheel
(He thinks he's wise as Aristotle).

His eyes are gazing at the stars
He spends like "skies the limit"
He's bound to burn his candle down
Ere maturity might dim it.

He knows the world is his alone
(However much remains)
His head is clamped with earphones
—And he's sitting on his brains.

Pal-in-drome

The palindrome's a line or word,
Don't know which way he's goin'
His head is 'zactly like his tail
Without much middle showin'.

If you should drive a palindrome
For better or for worse
You'd always find his forward
Is the same as his reverse.

The family of the palindrome
Is normal as can be;
There's Mom and Pop and Sis and Bub
Then there's the kook—that's me.

A Typical Typist

My typical typist types away
In her typical typist's chair
She types my topics without delay
Oh, she'd never think of asking for pay
She's the type of typist who cares.

She clickety-clacks through a typical day
And far into the typical night
Do you think she's the type who likes typing away?
Her feelings she typically won't betray
But—she types because *she* can't write.

A Gender Gem

I accept the fact that God is "He"
While locomotives and ships at sea
More often are described as "she."
Has anyone else ever wondered
In logic of rhythm or rhyme
How did nature become "Mother Nature"
And time become "Old Father Time"?

The Weather Guessers

These meteorologists cause me stress;
More often than not they casually guess
The kinds of weather the winds will bring
In winter, summer, autumn, or spring.

"Thirty percent chance of rain," they may say
But no rain pitter pats through the entire day
Then we know we were just in the 70 percent
And not in the 30 where the rain surely went.

They say we'll have snow or perhaps rain or sleet
Who knows, will the cold front advance or retreat?
And the "partly cloudy" they frequently say
Is the same as their "partly sunny" day.

But the paltry prediction most fickle, I fear
Though useless, I confess that it tickles my ear—
"There's a definite chance, if our crystal ball's right
That there probably won't be any sunshine tonight!"

Whale-Watch Tour

Ah yes, we sought the wily whale
But he showed neither hide nor tall
And then, the more to put us out
He showed us neither spray nor spout.

Still, the boat ride was a treat
The clambake mighty hard to beat;
We learned of history and realty riches
Of castles and demons and sinister witches.

From Oneonta to Salem and back
We never once got off the track
I'd describe this trip with one remark,
"A bus load of friends on a weekend lark".

Anni

We are happy to sing with you
Just to be part of the whoop-di-do
Small wonder that your rating's high
With audiences far and nigh
Your cast of thousands entertains
Yet the simple fact remains—

Your voice is vibrant with verve and dash
We struggle with interval and tone
Truth is, your concert would be a smash
—If you sang it entirely alone.

Susquehanna Chorus (1988)

We have sung the Broadway scene
Back and forth and in between
Is it possible we've really done it all?

After Hart, Berlin, and Kern are sung
What men of note are left among
The music-writing masters we recall?

Ah yes, there still are songs to sing
Melodies for remembering;
Let's not wait till spring to spread the news

That next year's treat will be a dandy
With music, sweet, of W.C. Handy—
"A night for the re-birthing of the blues."

How about:
    "Saint Louis Blues"
    "Basin Street Blues"
    "Beale Street Blues"
    "Blues in The Night"
    "I Get the Blues When It Rains"
    "Am I Blue?"

Jenny Kissed Me
—By Leigh Hunt

Jenny kissed me when we met,
Jumping from the chair she sat in.
Time, you thief who love to get
Sweets into your list, put that in.
Say I'm weary say I'm sad;
Say that health and wealth have missed me;
Say I'm growing old, but add—
Jenny kissed me!

Home with Mary
(Inspired by Leigh Hunt's "Jenny Kissed Me.")

Say I've failed my verse is sorry
Say I don't amount to much
Complexions paled, my locks are hoary;
I've reached the days of cane and crutch.

Say that I was skipped by fame
Memory's bad (old age is scary);
Recount my defects, mar my name
But add—that I rode home with Mary!

What! Already?

Old Father Time came around again
I didn't mind that so much, but when
He said those few days he'd placed in my folder
Had caused me to be a whole 'nother year older

I said to him, "Ol' Fella, let's make a deal
You know that you're only as old as you feel;
I'll swap you a *y* for an *e e n*
Then I can be seventeen again."

He just shook his head as he murmured, "No swap."
But I play every card in my hand 'fore I stop—
"I'll give you *t y* without making a trade
Then I'll gladly go back to the second grade."

Since Time Began

Time has a way of speeding by
Faster and faster as years do fly;
Folks say that there's no way to slow it.

Perhaps not, but my keen mind must try
To think of a way, a real do-or-die
Way to ground it, or kill it, or whoa it!

So I check each of my options well;
They are ever so few, I dread to tell
Which leads me to gripe and grouse.

A sudden brainstorn. Now I know
A way I can make time cease to go
—I'll unplug every clock in the house!

A Fitting End

My wife bought me a "fitted" shirt
And when she had me in it
It fitted very skinfully
If only for a minute!

And then its seams it quickly burst
By me then it was roundly cursed
The shirt stayed calm throughout the split
—*I* was the one who had the fit.

That's Me, All Right

Please forgive me
If I seem a little stubborn
And a little less than smart
(If you're looking for a perfect fool
I'll audition for the part);
If I seem unsympathetic
And my manner's rather crude
My mind is wandering somewhere
And I'm in a rotten mood;
My temper's rather short
While my diatribe is long
I know that I'm all right
The others all are wrong;
If I seem to be obnoxious
In the things I do and say
Forgive me, please forgive me
—I'm being myself today.

Success Story

Success! A commodity many have sought
Yet accomplished by ever so few
It can neither be begged nor borrowed nor bought
Mere money can't buy it for you.

To successfully serve, to fill human need
Is as high as a soul can aspire;
To labor with honor, conform to a creed
While revering a power higher.

But success is as empty as last year's bird's nest
Unless coupled with worthy endeavor
At times "unsuccessful" may even be best
Along with a definite "never."

Would we wish "all success" to a robber
A kidnapper or rapist or such?
How about an in-the-back stabber?
Of success, I'd wish none of them much.

Or when suicide's tried without success
To the desolate and utterly downed
Would one a future effort bless
With "Better luck next time around"?

"Success" of itself is a nebulous term
That can be either blessing or blot;
When I hear that a person's successful
I want to know—"At what?"

The Worm Turns

While spading in my garden
With a serious legal problem
I had to deal in no uncertain terms.

Invasion of privacy was displayed
Invasion was the role I played
The privacy? a wiggly angleworm's.

I turned his home right upside down
And dumped him, naked, on the ground
Exposed and bare for all the world to see.

He was really quite indignant
(And even tried to change his pigment)
As he registered complete distrust of me.

So I turned him back down under
Apologizing for my blunder
Hoping he'd forgive and wouldn't sue.

To plead ignorance or insanity
Would surely wound my vanity
Restitution was the human thing to do.

May he build more tunnels stately
I'm indebted to him greatly
Let's hope "happy" is the way the story ends.

For everybody knows that gardeners
And angleworms are mutual pardners
And needs must be the very best of friends.

Now I Remember

Forgetting was starting to cause me anguish
Then in a dentist's den, as I did languish
I read in a medical journal on memory
An opinion that seemed to make sense to me.

It recommended the using of rhymes
To help remember names, places, and times
And so I penned this little verse—
Forgetting would be so much worse.

If rhyming's the clue to the memory game
At least it should help me remember *my* name.

From Ay to Aye

Hey!
I'm Ray
In a rhyming way
There's the devil to pay
And the mice will play
When the kitty's away;
You don't have to stay
If it will spoil your day
You can swing and sway
Or display your sashay.
I'll continue to bray
'Cause my feet are clay
And come what may
When I'm old and gray
I still will say,
Hey! I'm Ray
—Aye.

Horsepital Report
(To Sheba, a horse I groomed for friends on vacation.)

Sheba's had intensive care
The while her head nurse wasn't there;

Nutrition, grooming, exercise
Fresh air under bright, blue skies.
Small wonder that she's feeling fine
With TLC why should she pine?

I care for her as best I'm able
And label her condition "stable".

Modern-Day Shaker
(On a sermon professing that people should be like salt.)

Your sermon contained much truth
With it, I can find no fault
But it cut like a serpent's tooth
I'll take it with a grain of salt.

Clapp Trap
(Another limerick.)

A foolish retiree named Clapp
Has traveled all over the map
He wound up at earth's end
Where he'd nary a friend
Like a rat in a Florida trap.

Greenhouse Absentee

The flowers have missed me
While I've been away
And some of them went to pot;
Some that were thirsty
Were driven to drink
While others were hungry a lot.

Nobody told them
How much they were loved
Nobody did much—right or wrong;
Nobody sprayed and nobody prayed
Or put them to bed with a song.

Man-to-Plant Monologue

Little plant, so calm and still
Your placid life-style, you fulfill
In days of beauty and repose
Serene and gentle as a rose.

Little plant, I envy you
Just sitting there the whole day through
While I must scurry 'round a lot
But, unlike you, don't have a pot.

Gift Wrap

Plain brown paper's what I choose
For 'voiding disappointment's blues
Lest you might say, morose and miffed,
"The wrapping's worth more than the gift."

Re-probate

Don't go to probate court alone
When settling an estate;
Take along your lawyer
A licensed reprobate.

Crime of the Month

"G‍UILTY OF S‍TATUTORY R‍APE"
So reads the garish headline.
I thought, *There must be some mistake
Or else the guy must be a flake
A sexual nut, a fruity cake;
He must be lower than a snake.
What sort of pervert would it take*
—For goodness' sake
To *do* that *to a statue?*

On Hypnosis

Post-hypnotic suggestion
Is a topic quite intense;
It can't be decently debated
While sitting on the fence.
With keen, in-depth perception
Of what is there to boast?
It couldn't take much talent
To hypnotize a *post*.

Happy Holidays

I just can't keep up with these special days
They come and go so fast
There are days for the flag and days of praise
And some for presidents past.

Anniversarys, birthdays, and firsts of the year
And a day for a Wednesday of Ash
A Good Friday, Saint Patrick's, and then *it's* here
—The day IRS takes our cash.

There are so many more it makes my head swim.
They have one for Mother and Father
But I'm sure, if you're thinking of more days for *him*
He'd say, "Hey, forget it, don't bother."

As for me, I'm confused in a strange sort of way
I got romantic on Groundhog Day
Slept right through Saint Valentine's
Gave thanks, almost any time
And while breaking 'most every holiday rule
I'm forever and always—an April Fool!

A Man for All Seasons

I love soft winds of springtime
And the sultry summer sun;
I love them 'cause they bring time
For happiness and fun.
I love the autumn woodlands
With its crimson and its gold;
I love all the passing seasons
—But winter leaves me cold.

Violence in the Garden

As I strolled through the garden
For which I care
Attack and survival
Were rampant there.
Cucumbers and squash
Were invaded by air;
Striped beetles and potato bugs
Getting their share.
It was Pearl Harbor day
For the grape and the rose;
The Japanese beetles
Had sneak-attacked those.
Still, the bees did *their* work—
As they buzzed all around
A bean strangled a tall-top onion
And wrestled it to the ground.

Down and In

When you're so deep in the hole
That you can't get out
And for losin' you just can't win;
No one will heed if you holler or shout
The lonely blues taunt you again.
Lady Luck has long gone
You've been fickled by fate
Then the best thing to do
Is just *hibernate.*
Happy Groundhog Day!

Dietary Preference?

Potato bugs eat the potatoes
Corn borers gnaw the corn
Cucumber bugs are chewing the cukes
'Round the clock from earliest morn.
Bean beetles are after the beans
Borers are spoiling the squash
If we don't get rid of tomato worms
We won't have any Prego sauce.
There are worms and bugs
Grubs, flies, and slugs
Eating every crop I'd protect
But in sixty years plus
Wresting food from the dust
I've not seen a *weed* beetle yet.

Greenhouse Plants and People

As we perform our daily toil
In pots we place the plants with soil
Then, on the bench we find a spot
In rows we space them—"pot to pot."

We Sunday to the banquet went
And found, by chance or by intent
Arranged in rows, I kid you not
Our friends, all sitting "pot to pot."

On Ambidexterity

Each day I survey folks I meet
In restaurant or bank or store
In laundromat or city street
Athletic field, at beach or shore

Although some few left-handed do
What others do with right
There's not enough left-handers
To put up a healthy fight
Outnumbered as they are, you see
By right-of-hand majority.
So here's my survey-based conclusion
When it comes to being deft
More folks are ambidextrous
With the right hand than the left.

Let It Ring

The telephone jangles but I don't run.
It seems to me that anyone
Who'd be on the phone
Won't know that I'm home.

The caller will know whom he didn't address
While I can speculate and guess
Who tried to call
And if the call is important, why then
Later the caller can call again.

Western Square Dance Class
(Dedicated, in appreciation, to Ken Hover, caller.)

When the dance breaks down
As dances often do
Nobody lends a hand
When we should square through;
We don't know which way to turn
And we don't know where to go
Right in the middle of a *do paso;*
When we find we're staring out
And we should be lookin' in
Our opposite is standing
Where we know we should have been.
It's not that we don't know
Our left foot from the right
Or that we've been goofin' off
Just a teenie bit tonight;
The answer's fairly simple
When you stop to read the signs
Somebody is confusin' us
And messin' up our minds.
BLAME IT ON THE CALLER
He's the one that's done it wrong
And he isn't even singin'
Our favorite song!!!

Sheba
(An equine friend.)

Sheba, queen though you may be
Though you may live in luxury
Are treated much like royalty
Still, you never high-hat me.

You've never lost the common touch
Your friends all love you very much;
Sheba, our love, surely, you did earn.
While we proffered food and caring
You your very self were sharing
And giving us *your* loving in return.

For a Ceramic Frog

Thank you for the perfect pet
Housebroke before I got her yet;
Requires neither pen nor stable
Don't tail-wag stuff from off the table;
She doesn't kick or scratch or bite
Or give me nightmares in the night;
She never growls, she never sighs
Nor barks, meows, nor whines nor cries.
The ever-enigmatic smile
Makes one forget the heart of tile;
Just sitting there in royal fashion
I'm sure she loves me with a passion.
She doesn't smell or bleed or sweat
This bestest pet I've ever met.

Energy Crisis

I got this great big bill
From the electric company.
I said, "There must be some mistake
They can't do that to me."
So I called them on the phone
And told them of my plight;
They promised me an expert
Would be there before the night
To check circuits and the meter
And to find out what's to blame
For making my electric bill
An inflationary shame.
With testers and computers
He traced my source of juice
And checked all the connections
To see if they were loose;
Appliances and breakers
He checked with stern intent
With all his mind he tried to find
Where all that current went.
—Then he found
A lead cord, without attachment
Was plugged in behind a door
And all that unharnessed voltage
Had just dripped out on the floor.
You may think that's very funny
But for us no cause for mirth
There was three hundred forty-two thousand
One hundred and twenty-six dollars' worth.

Ain't Technology Grand?

Let me tell you 'bout this labor-saving, wonderful machine
That we've put into our kitchen just to get our dishes clean.
We used to wash and dry them and then put them away
But that took such a lot of time from every busy day.

Now we wash and rinse the dishes
But we leave the cupboard bare;
We put the dishes in the washer
And let them tarry there
Till there's nothing left to eat on.

A crisis is impending so we turn on the machine
And it washes all those dishes we already had so clean.
The splishing and the splashing finally ceases by and by
So we wipe and dry the dishes that are not already dry;
Then we put them in the cupboard
Till that happy moment when
We put them on the table, just in time to start again.

Meanwhile, in our dream world of fantasies and wishes
We plan how best to spend the time
We used to use in washing dishes.

Enigma

I've heard why the chicken crosses the road
But did you ever hear anyone say
What's in the mind of a chicken
That only goes half the way?
After hours of cogitation
And wracking this brain of mine
That chicken was bound and determined
To lay it right on the line!

It's in There

Sooner or later there comes a time
When my wife will say, as if probing a crime
(And I will resist an urge to confess),
"How did this place get in such a mess?"

Whether garage or cellar, attic or den
There's more "stuff" there now then there used to be then
In bags and boxes, in cartons and crates
Who knows how that treasure accumulates?

Yet when I want to build or fix or repair
The junk that I need is so often right there;
So in answer to "How did we get such a mess?"
I reply, "I don't know, just lucky, I guess."

Hermit

I'm just an old hermit, way back in the woods
You may think I don't count for much;
Ah, but I do. With some products and goods
I'm the man with the perfect touch.

One shouldn't be judged by a life-style revealed
We're not all what we seem, you see
And when you see the words "hermetically sealed"
—Then you'll know it was sealed by *me*!

Condiment

Though I'm well seasoned, I am not
As some may think, a pepper pot.
The raging sea is where I'll be;
A salty character—that's me.

On Three-Letter Nonwords

PSC PCB VIP ASC
SCC BBC IRS IRA
DWI PBA POD DOA
ERA APB FBI GOP
MFP HUD CBS MVB
PDQ HRA NFL MTA
NBC SOP AMA ETC

If I get my hands on the SOB
Who invented abbreviations three
I'll choke him with an IUD
And as he heads off to eternity
I'll tell him he can GTH
And hope that by his ETA
He'll be declared a DOA.

Portrait of a Jogger

Every morning he's up early
To run his mile or two or five;
He'll keep his legs in good condition
His body strong, as long as he's alive.

Then he *drives* down to the office
He lives six blocks away;
After work he rides the golf cart
These athletes *have* to play.

But the payoff is the weekend
Mighty happenings come to pass;
Our hero *rides* his mower
Cutting his tiny plot of grass.

Another Bridge Builder

Then there was Andrew
A builder of bridges unique;
He built round ones and square ones
Some almost nowhere ones
And some that came up to a peak.
But he finally came to a miserable end
When after a lifetime with scarely a friend
A lifetime of spanning the rivers and ridges
One cold, lonely night, his end was in sight
—He just got too big for his bridges.

Nothing to Sneeze At

When people get sneezed on
At work or repose
They never say, "Hey!
Please cover your nose."
They always say, "Bless you"
As they offer their sleeve—
That's why it's more blessed
To give than receive.

Heir Apparent

There's no way to keep it a secret
No news media needs to leak it
It's obvious for all the world to see;
When a normally trim young lady
Is about to give birth to a baby
It's apparent she's a parent-to-be.

Apology

While browsing a secluded nook
I found this long-forgotten book
And greater still my cause to rue
Remembered, it belongs to you.
So your forgiveness I beseech
Recalling that in all and each
Of us there is a bent
To wrong, in spite of good intent.
Forgiveness is divine and grand;
Believing that you'll understand
If I should sometime need it, then
I'll ask to borrow it again.

Poetic Brevity

Poems long and lengthy
The bards of old did write;
There were elegies and epics
The reader to delight.
While I write more succinctly
For neither praise nor purse
Just truthfully and honestly
In short—terse verse.

A Fine Line

When I'd like to write lines
Most wonderfully bright
And the words turn out
Very dull and too trite
I review the sad lines
And I really don't mean them
I hope that my critics
Will read in between them.

On Self-Deprecation

Hey there, *you* "behind the door"
Don't be so modest, we know the score.
Of brains and personality
And sharp good looks, you've got all three.
You hit and run and make the play
And score the very nicest way.

In fact, you've talent without end
You'll never be without a friend;
You work and cook and look great; too;
You love and care, you're not just *you*.
You're "something else" and that's no lie;
You're *good* at everything you try.

Don't feel so sad "behind your door"
You got your share and plenty more.

Happy Medium

Let me tell your fortune—
I predict that you
Will have a happy holiday
And the reason that I do
Is—you're such a lovely person.
And I'd also like to say
May life be sweeter, brighter
With your every passing day.

(I further predict that next week
If you'll call me on the line
You then will speak to the friend you seek
—Call a little after nine.)

Hospitalized Again?

Them doctors ain't gonna find out nothin' new
So why not stop playing the jerk?
We figure the very best thing you can do
Is to get off your butt and come on back to work.

A Friend's Hemorrhoid Surgery

Oh, what a shame
What a miserable shame
That you should be paying a fee
To get reamed out;
When so many, no doubt
Would be glad to do it for FREE.

Expensive Care

Methinks, sir, that you are a bit of a knave
Taking your ease, while the rest of us slave.
But while nurses do hover, your wants to fulfill
Relax and enjoy it and don't ever spill
A drop of the pleasures that o'erflow your cup.
What a sneaky way to get all rested up.

Donor or Donee?

I-s-t, as a suffix, means "one who";
That's what we've been led to believe.
In terms of medical transplants
Does an organ*ist* give or receive?

Reluctant Patient

The doc said he'd do a lobotomy
He promised to incise with care;
I said, "Not a chance, I'll stay in my pants
—You won't find *my* brain down there."

It Only Hurts . . .

The local doctor soon gained fame
Both far and wide;
For the folks who came
To him for relief from sundry ills
He'd prescribe a weird assortment
Of palliative pills.

There were pills for the heart and also the liver
Pills for goose pimples and even for shiver
Pills for cramps and measles and gout
Pills to stop smoking and hair falling out
Pills for the fever and 'verticulosis
Pills for every possible diagnosis.

Small wonder then that he came to be
Known as the "Piller"
Of the community.

Surgery

There's a rumor going 'roun'
That a favorite in our town
Has had an operation that's a dilly
And we miss your smiling face;
While you're in that medic place
Our world is sunless, sorrowful, and chilly.

We'll be glad to have you back
No matter what you lack;
We'd rather have you nearer than afar.
Even if there *is* less of you
Must confess, we still will love you;
May we be among the first to see your scar?

Get Well Soon
(They removed your WHAT?)

We once had an "old tin lizzie."
When it got so it wouldn't run
We'd take it apart and put it together
And after the job was done
We'd always have some leftovers
Which we'd simply throw away.
You know that flivver never did wear out
Like the wonderful "one-hoss shay"
It just disappeared a bit at a time
Until one memorable day
There was nothing there, it was simply gone
Discarded—along the way.

Now I wouldn't say nor even suggest
That old car is a bit like you
Although there is an analogy here
We have to admit, that's true;
Both reached the point where no longer you'd run
Both were then of some parts bereft.
But don't worry, Elma, Baby—
You still have a great deal left.

Minor Surgery

My friend had an operation
On a part of his body he prized
Since I can't recall the name at all
I just say he was penalized.

I heard that the doctor botched it
Removed more than he ort;
Now the patient will operate on the doc—
The case is in *small* claims court.

Daylight Saving Time
(Explaining it to a youngster.)

You ask about daylight saving time?
Well, let me try to explain;
I know you'll think that it's crazy
Some of *us* think it's insane.

Early in the spring we sneak out of bed
In the deep, dark, dead of night
And set all the clocks an hour ahead;
It will hurry the morning light!

Everyone knows what everyone's done
And the clocks don't seem to mind;
Only the dependable, jolly, old sun
Has been left an hour behind.

In October, on a night especially black
We sneak out of bed at two;
This time we turn the clocks all *back*
And the *sun* doesn't know what we do.

So we call *that* daylight "saving" time
But when the year is finally done
Eight thousand seven hundred and sixty hours
Have fled—we weren't able to *save* even *one.*

Yet after it all, the sun still rises
And sets on its scheduled, orderly plan
Unruffled, unshaken by the silly surprises
And foolish foibles of man.

Blue

Any color that is blue
Gives a thing the proper hue.
Be it raiment, sky, or water
Or the ink beside the blotter
Blankets for an unborn child
Or blue iris, growing wild
Music or the mood I'm in, or
The haze that's mountain climbin'
Violets in a wooded nook
Bluebirds singing near the brook
Anything worthwhile, it's true
Deserves to be a shade of blue.

Sequel to "Blue"

Those lines once penned so long ago
Were truthful then, but now I know
There's room for *other* colors, too
And I have modified my view,
Some things are better *not* so blue
I'll try to name you just a few.
I'd rather that my grass was green
White snow creates a lovely scene
And yellow butter's only right
Red roses are a pretty sight
An orange a luscious orange should be
A brownie's brown, as you can see
Pink elephants needs must be pink
While memories are gold, I think.
Though blue is great—when all is said
I'd rather have my poems *read*.

Pen Pal

Woofers and foofoos we need not at all
To remind us of how much we care;
Though holidays, seasons, and governments fall
I'll be here—and you'll still be there.
The way that we feel keeps us pushing the pen
Instead of the old panic lever
'Cause sweethearts fall out
And married couples *do* doubt
But super pen pals are forever.

Ambition

Even when I was seven years old
I knew what I wanted to be;
The butcher, the baker, the candlestick maker
Held no attraction for me.

A cowboy, a cop, a hobo, a fop?
No future with them, could I see;
Wouldn't go for the forestry service
Even if I were a tree.

It had to be something that I could do best
So what did I choose to be?
A cookie scarfer par excellance
With someone like you, the scarfee.

Belle

Of all the ladies anywhere, you're the local belle
You 'peal the most, you toll, don't tell
And every time you start to swing
You're our favorite ding-a-ling.

Housewarming

May much joy and happiness
With thoughtful acts of tenderness
May quiet calm and gentle care
Pervade this home. May all who share
The warmth and comfort it extends
Be blest by God and loved by friends.

Driving Instruction

Don't try to teach your wife to drive
You'd be heading for a fall;
You'd be a mighty lucky fellow
If you could teach her a thing at all.

Floaters

Some (used-to-be) friends say
A water ballet
Is their favorite way to revel;
I really don't know
If they'll highlight the show
But they'll sure raise the water level.

To a Dog-Bitten Friend

Aside from being "man's best friend"
(And that doesn't say much for women)
A dog is a dog to the bitter end.
It's sad that *my* friends end up in stitches
When they get involved with those sons of bitches.

Key Man

In days of old
When knights were bold
And chastity belts were in style
The happiest face
To be found anyplace?
The locksmith with his broad, broad smile.

"Where's the Beef?"

The ground-beef patty was sizzling hot
When I paused to ask if he liked his lot.
His reply was brief and also droll
He said, "Don't interrupt me
—I'm on a roll."

Dodger-Mania

High in the bleachers, as I sat
I saw a little man
Dashing toward the entrance gate
—A rabid baseball fan.
"Hurry," I encouraged him enthusiastically,
"The Dodgers have three men on base."
"Which base?" cried he to me.

Odd Fellow

No! I don't find it very strange
Or hard to understand
Nor would I say your mind is incomplete;
It's only natural that you should wear
An old sock on your hand
And a pair of yellow mittens on your feet.

March Seventeenth

Saint Patrick's Day is here again
It bursts upon the scene;
If it's true "No man is an Ireland"
Then why are we all wearing green?

Hostess

The "hostess with the mostess"
Near a party is your spot;
There's no doubt that you're the hostess
The question is—with the mostess WHAT?

Unsolicited Wake-Up

When the telephone rings
At half past four
To tell me I can sleep no more
That's a call I call *obscene*
Malicious, malevolent, mangy, MEAN.

Pen-cil Pal

I notice by your letter
That your writing's black and blue;
I surely hope the same thing
Of the author isn't true.
I have always tried my darndest
And you know I always shall
To avoid inflicting bruises
On a pensive pencil pal.

Delayed Grand Opening

Spring arrived
In a great white package
Tied with a golden bow
Truly beautiful, and so
Lest winter's beauty we forget
Let's not open it
Just yet.

The Critic

I wrote some lilting lyrics
That I felt were pretty good;
I thought *They should be in a song
If only someone could.*
A songster then I quickly sought
He perused not overlong;
"Your lyrics are superb, my friend
—It's the *words* that are all wrong."

Compulsive Rhymer

It seems that each time
That I break out in rhyme
I'm blest with this terrible curse;
Be it blank or bright,
Free, serious, or light
I take a turn for the *verse*.

Just a Few More Limericks

At night when I can't go to sleep
I count Irish girls 'stead of sheep;
Those lasses are pretty
They're charmin' and witty
Then I dream that I'll have one to keep.

Heller

A happy young hippie named Heller
Thought that he was a very smart feller
Till his wife claimed her rights
To punch out his lights—
You should have heard Bill Heller beller.

. . . "and Touch Someone"

A lady a bit overweight
And a fat man went out on a date
When they danced to the fiddle
They touched in the middle—
The rest of them just had to wait.

Shoofly Pie

There once was a thoughtful fly
Who contemplated a pie
But his feet got all goo
And stuck there like glue;
He invented "pie in the sky."

On the Briny Deep

An Irish lad blest with the blarney
Embarked on a watery jarney;
"I'm not sea sick," cried he,
"I'm just sick of the sea
And I long for the gals of Killarney."

Jough Blough?

A windy young fellow named Jough
On a horn did constantly blough
For he said, "Don't you see
This music's in me—
So I blough with the flough for the dough."

Bush

A card shark whose name was Bush
Was wont to pinch girls on the tush;
He said, "It hurts them nice
It helps break the ice
And lifts up my libido a push."

Father's Day Is Forever

We know we love each other
By the good times we have had
And there's bound to be a bond
Between a daughter and a dad
But don't lavish gifts upon me
That at best provoke a shrug;
If you would express appreciation
—Just give me a heartfelt hug.

Soap-on-a-rope or ties or hose
Sweaters? I need none of those.
Jewelry, a watch, or a diamond pin?
None of these fit the mood I'm in.
What I'm trying to say in my clumsy way
These old heartstrings long for a tug.
You can make my day, chase the blues away
—Just give me a heartfelt hug.

Political Observation

Democrats are on the rise
Republicans should wane
Though I don't use a crystal ball
The prophecy is plain.
Symbolism tells it all
Elephants are near extinct;
Jackasses, already wall to wall
Daily wax more numerous, I think.

Part XII

Somewhat Personal

This group of poems is mostly of family and friends, along with a few reflecting my personal philosophy of life.

Character

Yes, I'm a "character," I guess
That's what some people say;
Don't worry 'bout their silly names
Or let them spoil my day.
Real people have been "characters"
Throughout all history;
I'd be nothing else but proud
If one of them were me.
"Character" is not a title
I would lightly shun
'Cause character's what one must have
To be one.

What's for Fun?

I lost my love for fishing
When I was five years old
I gave up treasure hunting
Due to scarcity of gold
Golfing is a nothing sport
Skiing leaves me cold
Skydiving is for youngsters
Who don't care for growing old
But
The years did treat me kindly
(No arthritis pain or gout)
And I've never lost my love for sex
—I've simply petered out!

Life-Style

Good health and zest for living
The best of life
To know the joy of giving
And of doing something nice
For someone, to be strewing
Happiness along life's pathway
Will bring life's happiness our way
And yet—
If life doesn't always
Turn out that way
A hope that is strong
Will carry the day
And loving together
We're sure to find
That happiness
Is a state of mind.

As Is

If we could change some of the things that are wrong
In this world of oppression and sin
We might wish for the fragile to feel more strong
And arrange for some losers to win;
We might even improve the face of the moon
Or perhaps we'd transpose a star
But no matter whatever the changes we'd make
We'd want *you—just as you are*

Advice

When I was just a little tyke
A-riding on my three-wheel trike
Folks used to give me free advice
To teach me how to live.

Little thought I gave it then
But now I've reached a moment when
Good council is appreciated
I accept the help they give.

I listen with an open mind
But ultimately, then I find
That having heard from all of these
I decide the issue as I please.

Appearances

I don't want to *appear* to be
A dude, a tourist, or jerk;
I don't want to be known as
A bigot, a chauvinist, or a shirk;
I don't want a wide reputation
As a thief, a cheat, or a corpse;
Those I don't want to be known as
And I *do* want to *be*
"None of the above," of course.

By Comparison

I have never been sold on growing old
Before my last song has been sung
So I hang out with folks who are *older*—
It makes *me* seem so young.

Roots

A favorite craze in recent days
Is the searching for ones ancestry;
We scramble around in the old family tree
Much like squirrels at nutting time
Gleaning the grains of genealogy
In ways methodical or sublime.

But as for me, no more I search
To satisfy raw curiosity;
My parents and forebears on farms did toil
On the land they could always be found.
It's spring—and time to till the soil;
My roots are firmly in the ground.

Ancestry and Destiny

My forebears, unknown emigrants
Chose this country for their own;
Adventure-bound they took a chance
And crossed the wild, tempestuous sea.
If they hadn't, I wonder who they would be?

They strove to perpetuate the race
In midwest's semiwilderness
(Wisconsin's sure a fertile place).
If my grandparents hadn't met
How could my parents do it yet?

My folks developed wanderlust.
When everyone was heading west
Our bumper read New York or Bust.
I wonder who I'd be today
If they had gone the other way?

As down life's road we swiftly go
These forks we reject or choose
Determine the person we are and so
If I'd made one different choice, I'd be
—Somebody else, instead of me.

Nature Lore

In the quiet confines of my garden
Both wisdom and caution I found
Potatoes with eyes to the future
And corn with an ear to the ground.

September Song

My garden now has run its course
And signs of age are showing
So soon returning to its source
It ripens more than growing.

Every stem, each plant, and vine
Has borne its fruit—
As I have mine.
With summer fading into fall
They, like me, await recall,
Recycling, end of line.

Very soon we'll meet the frost
While waiting winter's stormy blast
Well fortified for winter's cost
With memories of the summer past.

I see my garden through a glass
A mirror, reflecting eternity;
What I see and say of my garden
Is equally true of *me*!

The Trouble Is

You say you think children are trouble?
Shucks, mine are no trouble at all;
They don't give me a moment of bother
They don't even write or call.
They don't interrupt when I'm working
Or jangle my phone in the night;
Sometime I'd like to hear *something*
Even just, "Everything is all right!!"

Siblings

Of brothers and sisters several have I
We're scattered some miles apart
And each and everyone of them
Has a special place in my heart.

Though we have an occasional argument
We never begrudge or quibble
And I'm thankful *not* to have siblings
Who never learned how to sible.

Relatively Speaking

"You can choose your friends
But you can't choose your relatives."
Though I don't know who said that
There's no doubt that it's true
And aren't we the lucky ones
With relatives like you.

She Can't Understand It

My sister, bless her heart
Had some siblings from the start
And after that, she had some others;
Now, says she, she suffers stress
Perceiving that she has *one less*
Sister than do any of her brothers.

Sibling Rivalry? Not Us!*

Firstborn lays claim to be "number one"
Believing that makes him a favorite son
First in privilege, possessions, power, and praise
And the birth right that dates to biblical days.

Still, when the rest of us greeted the morn
We didn't ask questions like "Why was I born?"
But we're happy with each of our own destinies
Never asking "Why couldn't number one have been me?"

We *did* have concern for the one who came late
Thinking perhaps he'd had so long to wait
That the best material had all been depleted
Used up on us, born 'fore he was completed.

But last born with a smile brushed our worries aside
As with candid contentment and pardonable pride
With the wisdom of sages and prophetic insight
He said, "They had to keep doing it till they got it RIGHT!!"*

*When this last line was contributed by my youngest brother, Jim, I just had to write a verse in front of it.

RSVP

My absence really gives me pain
I'd hoped to see you all again
To hear the music, see old friends
Perhaps see if the voice still blends.
But now I'm doomed to disappointment
Here's the fly that's in my ointment:
After waiting all these months
I just can't be two places at wonths.

Seventy-five Years Ago: My Brother, Ted

"Hardly a man is now alive
Who remembers that famous day and year."
Longfellow wrote that long ago
It applies to many events we know
Like birthdays that continue to stack up high
As weeks and years do swiftly fly.
True, few there are who remember that date
When your journey began, your tryst with fate
But like twigs and roots on a family tree
That date means a lot to you and me.

It Takes One to Know One

There are those who know
When it's time to go.
Some folks know straight up
Some are wise enough to know
There's a slip twixt the lip and the cup
But however little or much we know
We all know one thing or another.
But nobody knows
That a guy is a *skunk*
Any better than his own brother.

Bob I

Ever since you were a kid
I tried to raise you, yes, I did;
Tried to help you on your way
To make you what you are today;
Taught you everything I knew
(It took me fifteen minutes, too);
Bound to make you be a man
A winner, not an "also ran";
Tried to keep you on the course
When necessary, I'd use force
Like, "You're the ship, man, I'm the rudder. . . . "
"Naw, he ain't heavy, he's my brudder."

Bob II

Some, for one reason or another
Have been embarrased by a brother
And some resent and some deny.
Ours is not to reason why
'Cause that's not true of you and me;
For although siblings we may be
For us, that means we're *family*!

Brotherly Greetings

I don't care what the others say
About the raucous, ribald life you've had;
Your terrible temper and disastrous disposition
May have brought you instant fame.
But a guy with a wonderful brother like me
Just can't be all that bad;
So have a helluva Happy Birthday
Just the same.

Brotherly Christmas Greeting

From a natural-born, intentional slob
To an SOB (that's Sweet Ol' Bob)—
Peace on earth the angels tell
Merry Christmas all to Hell!

Family Get-together
(With apologies to Kipling.)

"East is east and west is west
And never the twain shall meet."
Yet families *do* have reunions
A custom the miles can't defeat.

For blood is thicker than water
And we know from whence we sprung;
Brothers and sisters we ever remain
Even as when we were young.

"For there is neither east nor west
Border, nor breed, nor birth . . ."
When a common heritage glues us as kin
Though we're scattered all over the earth.

Higher Education
(*A parent's-eye view.*)

Nothing wins us knowledge
Like a boy or girl in college
No matter which the college one elects;
While the student tries for straight A's
The parents get their B.A.'s
In the modern liberal art of writing checks.

Still, we're happy we can do it
And we'll never ever rue it;
We're repaid in oh, so many ways.
We love you and we'll show it
'Cause almost before we know it
There will come an end to happy college days.

Firstborn

We expected imperfections
And planned on some corrections
Later when the others'd come along;
'Cause quality and pride
The first time that we tried
Was not the foremost thought
Our minds to cross.
We just thought we'd do our best
And, perhaps, if we were blest
The first one wouldn't be a total loss.
Beginner's luck was surely ours
Or help from supernatural powers
So we made no alterations
In that basic first design
No change in raw material
No revised assembly line
We just used the same equation
And continued to equate
For in spite of inexperience
And all sorts of interferience
Our experimental model
Turned out great!!!

Shadows*
(Apologies to Henry W. Longfellow.)

I have two little shadows
That go in and out with me
And how I'd do without them
Is more than I can see.

They're very, very like me
From their heels up to their head
And it's up to me to see
That they're sheltered, clothed, and fed.

You will notice if you watch them
That they're always on the go
And you simply can't describe them
With a synonym for *slow*.

Sometimes they come a-running
At my beck or at my call
But when they're into mischief
Then I can't find them at all.

In the morning very early
They come to wake me up;
All through the day they work and play
—You'd think that they would *drop*.

And at night those little shadows
When it's time to go to bed
Are full of vim and vigor—
While I, my friends, am *dead*.

---

*These were the first two, but a few short years later there were four of those little shadows and they had begun to overshadow their parents.

One Name for Four Sons

"Who steals my purse steals trash
But he who pilfers my good name
Steals that, which not enriches him
But leaves me poor indeed—" Shakespeare

They didn't really steal my name
I gave it to them—free
Each one of them was someone else
Yet each was part of me.

I'll only use it briefly
As I bear life's burdens and cares
And when I no longer need it
It's fitting that it should be theirs.

And their childrens' children's children
Will be honored to bear that name
Even as I and my forebears did
In the years before they came.

For a good name by shame unblemished.
Through generations of posterity
Will serve with pride and distinction
—As it did during ancestry.

The Childrens' Rowr
(Apologies to Robert Louis Stevenson.)

Between the dark and the daylight
About half past three or four
Comes a shattering of the silence
That is knows as the childrens ROWR

It defies all attempts at description
That weird globe-circling cry
And sleep is gone as you face the dawn
With that bloodshot look in your eye.

But as years go by, and they really do fly
Comes a time when you'd gladly endure
That wail of woe and your worries would go
—If you only knew where they were.

Unwritten Book

I really ought to write a book—
Doesn't everybody?
Would readers like to take a look
At my childhood, dull and shoddy?
But my parents loved us long and well
So I've no nasty things to tell
Or sludgy secrets to sell.
My folks were less than famous
And did nothing that would shame us;
They left me with a legacy so clean
If I write it, who would buy it?
So I'll never even try it;
Too bad my folks weren't *rottener* and *mean.*

To a Grandson Born on Christmas Eve

Welcome to our world
Imperfect, problem-ridden sphere
Though it may be;
It's the only one we have
And so it's yours. Away with doubt and fear
Go make it what you will.
It's long past time that someone
Made the changes that somehow
Have seemed always to elude us. Still
It's not too late to save us from ourselves
And hopes ride high and set the sky aglow
Even as it happened
On that Christmas long ago.

Aaron—Plus One

We often like to think of the good, old-fashioned days
When we celebrated Christmas in less sophisticated ways
And yet when we remember that a babe was born in love
Things haven't changed so very much, the same stars shine above
And hope still springs eternal for peace and happiness;
The same God has us in his grasp, and he alone can bless.

Gift List
(For all our families.)

For all those wonderful people on earth
Related to us by an act of birth;
Peace of mind, good health, a way to live
And all the love a dad and mom
A grandpa and grandma can give.

For a Friend

The prophet's dream has been answered
God's blessings have come without end;
No gift more wonderful can he bestow
Than to be blest with a real true friend.

Family

I was climbing around
In an old family tree
But those long-ago names
Didn't mean much to me
So I turned to the limbs of today.

And there I found Alex and Neelie
To make the heart sing and do jigs;
That old family tree
Means a lot more to me
Since they became some of the twigs.

Young Bill

Such a short, short time
Was the while you grew
So tall. We should have known
You'd soon be through
With high school, and now
We wish you all the best.
We pray that your life
Will be truly blest;
That you'll make of your life
The most you can
As you travel the road
To becoming a man.

Young Graduate

It never was easy
To be young, then or now.
Often it's tough
To do the best you know how;
You're going to win some
And perhaps lose a few
But don't let it down you
Or make you feel blue.
There'll be things that you can't
And some that you *can;*
Today you take a big stride
Toward being a man.

Graduation Gift

Young friend, this is really not for you
But for your friend Ed. Don't ask "Ed, who?"
Ed-ucation, that's your friend
Who'll help you learn and then will send
You into a world of take and give—
Equipped to serve and love and live.

Paperboy

Paperboys come short or tall
Some come with smiles that are wall to wall
Some come with substitute sister or brother
Or, sometimes, even with fathers or mothers
Some come with long hair, some with curly
Some come late and some come early
What we started to say, because it's true
—It's great having a paperboy like you.

To Neglected Friends

Maybe you think that we just don't care
As we breathlessly rush from the here to the there;
Of all sad words of tongues or pens
The saddest are these, "They neglected their friends."
But don't judge us too harshly, to be busy's no *crime*
And we bless you and love you—*whenever there's time!!!*

A Grandad's Dilemma

My family in the aggregate
Totaled four sons, that was great;
Just enough for what I'd need
To perpetuate my name and seed.

But now my sons have children, too;
What's a poor grandad to do?
How can I, whose sons were four
Encourage them to have no more—
To limit
While the people explosion lasts
Their progeny
To two and two-tenths baby blasts?

Sorry Situation

"Of all sad words of tongue or pen"
Some of the saddest, I think
Are, while writing a letter to a friend—
"My pen ran out of ink."

Logic to Live By

A grandpa sat in his burn-scarred chair
His cigarette was lit;
He coughed while the blue smoke filled the air
As he thought, *I just can't quit.*

He knew heart disease or lung cancer
Would shorten his life quite a bit
But be mumbled his usual answer,
"Don't nag me, I just can't quit."

Then his little granddaughter came near
And put her small hand on his knee,
"Grandpa, I love you a terrible lot;
Please, Grandpa, don't you love me?"

"Of course, I love you, Child. How could you doubt?
Can I really believe my ears?"
"Then why don't you throw the cigarettes out
So you can love me some *extra* years?

"For the years, you'd waste so lightly
With 'Sometime we all must die,'
Are my years too, and without you
There'll be no 'you and I.'

Because of what you mean to us
Your wisdom and your smile
My folks and I would like to try
To keep you for a while."

The old man snuffed out his cigarette
And wiped his eyes a bit,
"You just gave me the perfect reason
And, by gosh! *I'm gonna quit!*"

If you're a dedicated smoker
Vow by stars that shine above you
Though you might not quit to save *your* life
That you'll quit for those who love you.

Autobiography in a Nutshell

When I was just an embryo
And Nature said, "It's time to go"
I said, "I'm not sure, I don't know
But I'll try it for a while."

A few years later, off to school
They said, "Go on, don't be a fool."
I said, "Okay, if that's the rule
I'll try it for a while."

I went to work (avoiding crime)
A fulltime job took all my time.
The pay was worth the sweat and grime;
I tried it for a while.

When I was asked to love and marry
I always said, "Oh, let's not tarry."
I guess I wasn't very wary;
I'd try it for a while.

To be a father was I ready?
Take it easy, fella, steady.
This experience is so heady
"I'll try it for a while."

Grandfathering was just my style;
Grandchildren know ways to beguile.
They brought me many a happy smile;
I'm glad I tried it for a while.

Retirement caught me unaware;
What would I do with time to spare?
I find there's much to do and dare;
I'll try it for a while.

It won't be long before I'll fail
And when I reach "end of the trail"
The seas of life no more to sail—
Just say, "HE TRIED IT FOR A WHILE"

Reincarnation? Can it be
A second chance for you and me?
Of death—can it be said that "He
Just tried it for a while?"

Occupational Hazards

A good job is HARD to find
There are none that will satisfy;
Something is wrong with most every one
"Beware, all ye who apply."
Dishwashing was such a frustrating job
I washed them all clean, but then
They got all dirty all over again
'Fore I could count to ten;
I put in some time on the railroad
Heading down the wrong track
The engine and I ran out of steam
And we never got it back;
So I applied for work as a mailman
They were only hiring girls;
When I was a cashew salesman
I heard, "Nuts are only for squirrels;"
On the job for "Stove Top Stuffing"
I didn't have the right stuff;
Lost a job making GE light bulbs
'Cause *I* wasn't bright enough;
Then I tried doughnut making
But they all came out full of holes;
Once I was an entertainer
And played several interesting roles;
When I portrayed a crazy professor
Everyone thought I was daft;
I was cast as a clever comedian
But folks just laughed and laughed;
In a plant, I was running a drill press
But that turned out to be boring;
Didn't want a job far beneath me
So I gave up laying flooring;

Moving up, I was papering ceilings
But there was too much overhead;
Drove a hearse for a funeral director
My passengers all arrived dead;
Turning my hand to inventing
I thought it would be a snap
But I never perfected my very first one—
A mouse that could catch a trap;
I never dared to try teaching
Although a B.S. I did earn
Scared of those huge malpractice suits
For something somebody might learn.
So you see
There's no *perfect* job or vocation
To which I might brightly aspire;
For me there's no *other* solution
I'm just gonna quit and *retire*!!

Postal Problem

You postal people have earned my ire
And this lament did thus inspire
You bring my circs and bills and flyers
All paper to stoke my trash-can fires
But where are the letters we hold so dear
From friends and family, far and near?
Have you thrown them away with the office waste?
Or lost them enroute in your reckless haste?

No need to brave showers and sleet or hail
Unless you bring us some *first-class* mail
You can save the circs till day after tomorrow
As for bills, I'll postpone the day I borrow
What we need is some letters from family or friend
The kind of mail that loved ones send.

So, mailman, I hope that my message got through
It's *first-class* mail that we want from you;
Just in case your mind or you memory fail
I'll spell it for you—*first-class* m-a-l-e *mail.*

To Friends Departing

Every now and then with a sadness in the heart
And a sense of loss that's awfully hard to hide
The time arrives when best of friends must part;
It's a fact of life we face, "whate'er betide."

Let's blend our gentle voices in "Blest Be the Tie That Binds"
Though the parting's almost more than we can bear;
You'll be with us, friends forever, in our thoughts and on our
    minds.
Our "Best Wishes" will go with you—everywhere.

To a Friend

When I shall run my fortune through
To balance life's long bank account
I shall not, as the misers do
In money seek some large amount
But I shall claim those treasures which
Such sordid souls can't comprehend
In countless ways God made me rich
It was my luck to be your friend.

Some there must be with wealth and fame
To boast their selfish paltry deeds
A privilege man sorely needs;
A gentler blessing God bestowed
On me unto the journey's end
To share the burden and the road
It was my luck to be your friend.

Brave gentle soul, my life has run
Through kindly channels and serene
In all that I have ever done
I've had your strength on which to lean;
In that, I'm richer far than they
Who have but yellow gold to spend
For I can proudly state today
It was my luck to be your friend.

Farewell to Special Friends

When friends must part as they often do
There's a sorrow we can't deny
That fills the heart and makes us blue
We can't help it, however we try.

Still, we wish them the best, as they go their way
And their new home is blest by our prayers today;
We say our farewells as we smile through the pain
We know that our loss will be somebody's gain.

Special Friends' Special Anniversary

Twenty-five years is not very long
In God's so masterful plan
But twenty-five years is a real milestone
In the life of a woman and man.

Twenty-five years of loving and care
Twenty-five years of each "being there"
Twenty-five years of lives intertwined
Twenty-five years of those ties that bind.

What miracle has made love grow
To merit such marital success?
I frankly admit that's a thing I don't know
Just years of "Just lucky, I guess."

And for some of those years
We, too, have been blest
Since God gave us, as friends
Two of the best.

Good-bye to Good Friends

Far, far too brief, the time we had with you
And yet, somehow, we feel we made the most of it;
We forged some friendships that were strong and true
Accomplishments we've had, without a boast of it.
Recalling laughter and good fellowship of all kinds
Our happiness and joys seem infinite;
Discussions when we mingled hearts and minds
We'll not forget but treasure every minute.

Let's not be sorry then or sad
As we our charted destiny fulfill;
We thank you, God, for blessings we have had
And for a future patterned to your will.
So fare thee well and may God bless
The very best for you our prayers implore;
Your new friends will not love you less
Because we love you more.

Chosen

My friends, Walt and Henrietta
Have been married for quite a spell;
I don't know much 'bout their marital bliss
And perhaps its just as well.
Though I've known some "hen-pecked" husbands
And have heard them moan and groan
Walt is the only Henrietta-picked husband
That I've ever really known.

Donor's Prayer*

Now I lay me down to bleed
And pray that one in direst need
At a time when gloom and despair are rife
Will receive this gift of love and life.

*As a thirteen-gallon-plus donor, it could be said that my heart is in the blood-donor program. Likewise, the Literacy Volunteers of America program has also captured my attention.

Blood Bank Deposit

I'm making a shrewd investment
It seems mighty smart to me
To deposit what I don't need today
In no-risk, high-yield security.

The dividends are the greatest
An elation and peace of mind
A feeling of inner contentment
That's not ever easy to find

And the satisfaction of knowing
This deposit may save a life
Whether stranger or family loved one
A friend, a child, or a wife.

It's a joy to be a blood "donor"
With this gift for humanity;
From a strictly selfish viewpoint
I might sometime be a "*donee.*"

Preteaching Reflections of a Volunteer Reading Tutor

Why am I practicing alphabet
After so many years are through?
I learned it well during "show and tell"
Back in nineteen twenty-two!
It's been said "Life begins at forty"
If by chance you're still alve;
Could it also be a reality—
Second childhood at sixty-five?

Five Gifts

If per chance it should fall to me
To choose five gifts for humanity
The first I'd choose is faith, then love
Then peace, long symbolized by a dove;
Good health would be my number four
So quickly we're down to one gift more.
What be the final gift I'd send?
—To be able to *read* and comprehend.

Bean Burner

> If you're the type that loves to take the curves and corners of life on two wheels you'll be better off with a bicycle or motorcycle than with an automobile.
> —from Groves' Laws

We've a motorcycle and a van
A three-speed bike and a car
Most of them will take us fast
And some will take us far
Some run on fuels unleaded
There's regular for the rest, but
I've checked mileage per the gallon
And the bicycle is the best.

While all the others guzzle gas
In great big gulps it seems
The bike moves swiftly down the road
Propelled by good old beans;
Two wheels and good unleaded beans*
Is the healthy, smart solution
—No costly oil and fuel bills
—No provable pollution.

*Why unleaded beans instead of regular?
   Anyone knows if you're going to get any speed out of a bicycle, you have to "get the lead out!"

Motorcycling

The concrete reels beneath the wheels
The wind is fresh on my cheek
Raw power exists in the twist of the wrist
To the motor, the chain, and the sprocket
Exhilaration and exuberance ride high and persist
Like we're riding an earthbound rocket
Almost it seems like we're flying.
But there are problems that flying brings
And we're not ready to head for the sky
Not quite ready for heavenly things.
Though this little beauty can fly
It was never equipped with wings
—And neither am I.

My Alibi

The bravest, wisest, smartest man
In all of history
Was chosen as the pattern
For what was to be ME.

The scientist was clever.
'Twas thought that he alone
Could produce from that old blueprint
A single living clone.

But errors oft do happen
In the plans of mice and men
And no human has the answers
To the why and where and when.

So when the end result they viewed
My parents wore a frown.
"What went wrong?" they cried in grief.
"You've really let us down."

The scientist just shook his head
And headed back to town;
"Aha! You wanted *clone*," he said.
"I read that word as *clown*."

The Class of '34
(For a fifty-year reunion.)

Spawned in the depths of the first "great" war
Were we, to be the class of thirty-four;
We knew that times were changing, but
We didn't know how fast.
"Horse and buggy days" were gone
But would the love of auto's last?
And we had barely learned to fly
Jetliners were a dream.
Who thought that we'd run out of gas?
Or the railroads out of steam?

We had our "great" depression;
Our high school years we spent
In the hallowed halls of learning
Wondering where the "good times" went.
Then we had our own "great" war
And as past patriots have done it
We did our bit—except for death
Nobody quit
And presumably we won it.

Our members have served humanity
In all aspects of economy;
In government and industry
Our talents, time, and toil
Were brought to bear
Whenever and where're
A need arose.
And as our lives, we lived apace
We did our share to propagate the race.

Now of that half century of years
Embellished by our memories, smiles, and tears
Let this be said—
"We lived and learned and loved
The while those years did pass;
Of 1934 *we were the CLASS!!*"

Class Reunion
(Fifty-three years later.)

Should auld acquaintance be forgot
Of days that we hold dear
There's gold in those old memories
And we're mining some right here.

Remembering days of youth and school
Recalling classroom fun
School friends will be forever friends
While songs may still be sung.

Harmonic Convergence?

No one had ever explained to me
What "harmonic convergence" might possibly be
And so for myself I figured it out
By word derivation. I haven't a doubt
That "harmonic convergence" in its final dimension
Just must be a mouth-organ players' convention.

Unlikely Listener

A listener you'd like to be known as?
That doesn't quite fit your style.
Small wonder that just the mere mention
Provokes a guffaw or a smile.

For while others were ranting and raving
You did not stand apart from the crowd.
If you'll pardon a keen observation
Methinks, sir, you listen too *loud.*

A listener you'd like to be known as?
I'll try to smother a laugh.
Perhaps, NOW HE LISTENS would be
—A fitting epitaph.

Nate-urally

A lady who'd been here and there
With a friend named Nate had an affair
She said, "No ifs, ands, or maybe
Nate, this is *your* baby."
The others were pre-Nate-al care.

Fringe Benefit

You think that I have retired?
Really I'm working full time
I've not a moment for loafing
Or to write an occasional rhyme.
There's this little place on the edge of town
A garden, garage, and a house
A piece of lawn, some shrubs and trees
It's owned by a man and his spouse.
I'm caretaker and night watchman
The gardener and handyman;
I'm on call twenty-four hours
And I do everything that I can.
Though I never get paid in wages
Still, it's a wonderful life;
The owner and I are inseparable
—And I go to bed with his wife.

Things I Believe
(Though I've never seen them.)

The air we breathe and all that's in it
Time, each fleeting precious minute
Atoms and the raging wind
The constitution on the head of a pin

George Washington and Bunker Hill
Chromosomes and chlorophyl
Sex and sin and, yes, the pill
Viruses and searing pain
My heart, my soul, my so-so brain

Love and hate and mixed emotions
The force that moves the restless oceans
Vitamins and calories
The know-how of the honey bees
Corpuscles and gravity
Hormones and electricity

Sounds transmitted through the air
Voices, traveling a wire bare
The caffeine in my cup of tea
"Someone up there" who cares for me
Outer space concludes *my* list;
Make your own of things I've missed.

On Selling the Grange

You say, sir,, "The Grange is not for me!"
Then you don't know us well, because you see
Grange is a word that means neighbors and friends
Good, honest folk; our country depends
On Grange families, in good times or bad
To make these the best days that we've ever have.

Our roots and traditions have stood time's stern test
We appreciate all with which we've been blest
We keep love of country in mind and in heart
When a job's to be done, we each do our part;
In short, we're at home in America's mainstream
And would like *all* to share the American dream.

"I'm no farmer," you say. Well, *that's* not required
Our jobs vary widely, *some* of us are retired;
Yet agriculture holds interest for *you* and for *me*
'Cause we both like to eat and have prosperity.
Our nation's economy can't thrive very long
Unless agriculture is healthy and strong.

So I urge you, my friend, to take pen in hand
And sign on as one who loves this great land;
You'll find being a Granger a worthwhile endeavor
As we go building bridges from here to forever.
It's the happiest contract you'll ever arrange
—Friends are waiting to welcome you into the Grange.

Old Timer's Olympics

I never will run in the Olympics for fun
(One mustn't be paid, I am told)
The mile, the four hundred, the hurdles, and high jump
Are just medals for others to hold.

Some will vault with a pole or toward a far goal
Hurl the javelin, discus or shot
While I, from afar, will just wish on a star
Or be throwing the bull, like as not.

Yes, I know I'm too old for the bronze and the gold
The silver is all in my hair
Still, there are honors I'll vie for and probably die for
In trying to win a fair share.

For the titles I'm seeking are, generally speaking
Not conferred until after life's end;
They are "all-around world class" HUSBAND
FATHER, GRANDFATHER, AND FRIEND.

Runner

Always keep running as long as you may
There will always be plenty who crawl
Always run *toward* something never *away*
And you'll ever stand swift and tall.

Keep running as long as life remains
And when that life is gone
The ear of the fallen will catch the strains
Of others who still run on.

Not to Worry

A friend has many worries
And among his deathly fears
Is concern that stark heart failure
May terminate his years.

I reassure him often
And try to let him know
It's a perfect happy ending
To escape this life of woe.

If worries we *must* have
Let brain failure crease our brow
Heart failures in the future
Brain failures here and now.

In making a bad decision
Or saying a thoughtless word
In committing an unkind act
Or relying on something heard
In failing to get involved
When the heart says that we should
Interfering when we should stay aloof
Or doing less than we could.

Heart failure? A once in a lifetime
Leads to the heavenly way;
Brain failure is a chronic illness
We suffer most every day.

We'll Never Get Out of Here Alive or I'll Go Quietly

I heard this guy on the radio
Say they would do this terrific show
That would last for hours or even days
To drum up money to find the ways
To stamp out forever, with consumate ease
The "number-one killer" called heart disease.

Well, don't do us any favors, my friend
For each of us must find a way to end
And no other method under the sun
Is worthy of being our "number one."

'Cause cancer's fraught with pain and woe.
Accidents? What a sad way to go.
And certainly death by knife or gun
Should never be our "number one."

So I say, "Mr. D.J., have your fun
But please don't stamp out our 'number one';"
We'll pray when we're tolled by Heaven's bell
That heart disease is alive and well.

Unemployed

At first he stood up straight and tall
So certain that he'd get a call
Confident, though times were hard
That not for long he'd be discard.
He told himself that time would tell
They'd need the skills he knew so well
An upturn soon would come to pass
They'd need his service and his class;
Though bleek might be the working scene
He'd come through days when times were lean.
No robot he had ever known
Could take the place of flesh and bone.

But days and weeks have passed and still
No vacancies he's asked to fill;
No longer does he have his pride
He's sick and weak and limp inside
He thinks of jobs he once enjoyed
—This sex organ that's unemployed.

Final Curtain

> *All the world's a stage and all the men and women merely players: They have their exits and their entrances; and one man in his time plays many parts.*
> —*Shakespeare*
> *As You Like It*

The bard was right. We greet the light
Our entrance is accomplished
We strut or slog or creep or jog
Our brief time upon life's stage
And *sometime* we must exit
At an old or youthful age.
Our entrance was not of our choice
Our roles the whim of destiny
Decided by some other voice
As our acts uncurtain endlessly
And then the *exit*. Oh, Lord, let it be neat
No stage fright, no forgotten lines
No loitering, no stumbing feet;
Lord, let our exit be with CLASS
—Not while we're falling on our *face*.

Finally, Freedom

I searched for freedom as a child
But free I could not be;
Adults had cornered freedom
They had it up a tree.

Then when I reached adulthood
You think that I was free?
No! I was bound and shackled
To two jobs, a home, and family.

It's what I wanted, mind you
Though the strain was hard to bear
For freedom still eluded me
While I searched everywhere.

Now as death approaches
With prophetic clarity
I know that with life's passing
—I'll then be truly free.

Reassessing Retirement

I can't run as fast as I used to
The years must be gaining on me
My biceps have shrunk, my hair has grown thin
And I've got a bad catch in my knee.
Yet I feel independent and healthy
No need to be put on the shelf
I can dress and go to the bathroom
And I even can feed myself.

But nobody wants my opinion
My presence or even my time;
I never dreamed being past sixty
Would be such a terrible crime.
Lord, I don't want to be just a burden
Want to help with the chores here below
If *retire* means from the whole human race
—Take me, Lord, I'm ready to go.

Uncommon Sense

With age, they say, the senses pale
And one must learn to play the part
When hearing and the eyesight fail
Of being old but not too smart.

Well, though I'm getting older, too
A little slower when I move
My eyes are fine for taking a dim view
Of the many things I disapprove.

And if my hearing's not too keen
I don't have to half pretend
I didn't hear the gossip mean
When someone tries my ear to bend.

My sense of smell's the best of all
It's good enough my food to savor;
At table I can have a ball
Nosing out each special flavor.

Still, not *too* good, as I compare
With those with keener sense, methinks
They go around with nose in air
Saying, "The whole world stinks."

So I'm thankful for the ways I'm blest
Though quite an ordinary fellow;
I age no faster than the rest
And I'm not duller—just more mellow.

Waiting Again

I waited only nine lonely months
Before I entered life's door;
Headfirst I burst on the bustling scene
I'd never been there before.

Later on I waited for people or things
Some arrived and some *never* came;
I even got used to waiting in line
When *that* was the name of the game.

Now that the good life is over and gone
I'm ready to meet my fate;
Twilight never fails to follow a dawn
So why should *I* have to wait?

Versatile Verse-a-Pile

As leaves are scattered by the wind
Just so by family and by friend
My verses have been spread around
And like bright leaves upon the ground
Each has served in some small way
To brighten an otherwise dismal day;
Perhaps, if like leaves, we can compost them, then
From their utter decay we may profit again.

A Man of All Seasons

Born into the springtime
My life was in its spring
With a happy, hopeful boyhood
And a heart that's born to sing.

Like "a tree by the river of waters"
The summertime I knew
Brought both career and family
One prospered while one grew.

The autumn years were mellow
And brought both joy and pride
As our children chose their own careers
And took life's gifts in stride.

Now winter fast approaches
And it doesn't seem so cold
With wonderfully warm memories
Of loves we have and hold.

We know spring will be coming
And although we won't be there
Our spirit will be present
With grandchildren everywhere.

So let us have our winter
Each season we've been blest
Perhaps we'll have a mild one
—And then eternal rest.

The Time Is Coming

There comes a time in the life of a man
When he's done just about all he can
He's said his say and written his line
And tried to live up to his zodiac sign
He has run his race, his song's been song
He's thankful for friends he has lived among
So he surrenders with grace and nary a curse
And his grandaughter takes over writing his verse.

Last Rights

Unknown, unknowing
Came I here
My time and place
Undetermined by me
Unchosen my family
And my race
To live an unknown destiny.
My leaving, too
Is mystery

The how, the where
Just when and why
Without an omen or a sign
I only pray—
Don't let me stay
Beyond my time.

Premonition

If I should be the first to go
Please don't cry or let grief show
'Cause I'll be doing fine, you'll know
Up above or down below.
Heaven's just so very sweet
But if, perchance, we never meet
There, please don't be dismayed
'Cause you'll know I can make the grade
And that I came in from the cold
To out argue the devil
And that I stayed to hold my own
Against any sinner Hell can *hold*.
Yet if, as some folk's think, it's true
That life may return for me and you
Look for a kid on happy wheels
That shows the friendly way he feels;
With a heart full of love
A face full of smile, not too much class
Just a touch of style
Who somehow knows what love can do
And know that love will be for you.

Swan Song

Looking down life's lonely road
Or in a crystal ball
I see no future there for me
Except one final call.

At seventeen I didn't know
What I would be or do
At seventy whate'er the gain
I know that it is through.

Sometimes I lost but
More often I won;
It's last out in the ninth
The race has been run.

And neither would I slow or stop
The course of destiny
But swiftly let Death have its way
As it was meant to be.

No more work have I nor a battle cry
No challenge is there to be met;
I only owe one life to Death
—It's time to pay the debt.

I'll Go—but Not Voluntarily

Isn't it strange that so many
Of the better things that have happened
To me in the course of a lifetime
Came about in spite of misgivings
And feelings of dismay? From my very birth
I fought and struggled all the way and braced
My feet to no avail. Relentlessly
Some mystic force kept prodding me
Along the trail to fulfillment and a final peace
That comes when life and breath shall cease.
Consistent to the very end, I'll fight
Until that final breath, when I'll embark
Reluctantly, on life's last great adventure—death.

Part XIII

More Truth than Poetry

Though in a prose style rather than verse, hopefully the following will make a contribution in a philosophical or humorous vein.

Who Is Poor?

Christians are exhorted to help, to share with or to otherwise befriend the poor, but who are "the poor?"

Some families, I know, who are presumed to be doing well financially have no time for family activities or even for meals together. Life is work and sleep and passing by.

In contrast, a family whose members are recipients of "welfare" has *time*: twenty-four hours each day to be together, to spend as they please in family activities or personal interests. *Who* is poor?

A man considered by others as "well to do" can't enjoy his meals due to stomach problems, can't sleep due to financial worries. . . . Another who does hard physical labor for small pay eats zestfully, enjoys his food, and sleeps peacefully though he has no accumulated wealth. *Who* is poor?

A woman who has all the "comforts" money can buy—a nice home, automobile, wardrobe, and money for anything she desires—is unhappy. She believes her husband is unfaithful. Their marital relationship has disintegrated and lacks meaning and love. *Who* is poor?

When we were youngsters growing up in the Great Depression, we knew some childless folks who had money. They were considered to be wealthy. Our parents had eight children. We never saw any money, so I guess we were "poor," but we didn't know it. Our family had love, multiplied by ten. *Who* is poor? A quotation by George Santayana seems appropriate here: "What riches have you, that you deem me poor? Or what large comfort that you call me sad?"

Speaking for myself, some blessings for which I am grateful include the satisfaction that derives from hard work and knowing that a job was well done, plus excellent early training in developing a set of values. Add to this, I am grateful for having had the advantage of starting from *poverty.*

Parable of a Strike

"What is a strike?" you ask. And I say to you, "A strike is like a honey bee that gathers nectar from a blossom for honey to feed the hive. Then the bee discovers that it is pollinating the blossom and that the blossom cannot survive without this service. So he says, 'Look here, Flower, I'm doing you a favor by harvesting your nectar. You can't exist without me, so give me twice as much nectar or I will no longer provide my services and you will perish. Meanwhile, I will not gather any nectar at all until you agree to provide the amount that I demand.'"

Of course, the poor blossom cannot surrender more nectar because the honey bee is already taking all there is, and without the vital pollination it soon becomes an extinct species. As for the honey bee, he, too, is doomed to die of starvation for lack of the nectar he deigned to harvest.

Hence, both the blossom and the bee are unable to survive except in coexistence, working together—each in his own capacity—for mutual benefit.

Fortunately, *most* of God's creations never go "on strike."

Portrait of a Failure

I'm a failure, a self-confessed failure, but a failure nonetheless.
Oh, I've managed to survive through our depressions and the inflationary periods (up to now). I have a wonderful wife; a house with lawn, garage, and garden; and enough acreage left over to make a burdock patch. I have as good a car as I care to own.
I'm fortunate in having for a family some very special people, and also fortunate that mine is a two-fold family with a double group of special people, including a host of special grandchildren.
I've enjoyed better-than-average good health and have worked steadily at an interesting and challenging job for thirty-five years, with reasonably satisfying advancement, and I anticipate a happy retirement situation .
Oh, there is much for which to be thankful, and by many people's standards, I might be considered a success— but I'm a failure. The one I love smokes, and *I* can't stop smoking for *her.* I'm a failure—

Retirement: Sugar-coated Unemployment*

Retirement! It is no less odious a form of unemployment, despite its insidious nature and its reputation for being a goal in everyone's dream of the misnamed "golden years." The reality is that in the view of any corporation, agency, or society in general, there is no longer any "worth" for the retired husband. He is a piece of dead wood to society, a disaster to Medicare, a liability to Social Security programs, and the most expendable of our population. He is a totally nonproductive burden on the backs of the comparatively few employed and working persons.

His family has grown and flown. In this period of crisis, fortunate indeed is the man whose wife believes in his worth, at a time when his own self-esteem is lower than a whale's turd.

*This view of retirement was inspired by a newspaper article on unemployment. The harsh opinion depicted here, was subsequently softened and modified by this writer, after retirement had settled in.

Memories of Youth
(A vignette.)

During sweet-corn season we picked a lot of corn for the city folk who drove down to get it *fresh*. While we were picking the corn, they often admired my mother's flower bed, with good reason. My brother Bob drew the assignment, and when he returned with an armful of assorted, gorgeous blooms, he was told, "Those are positively beautiful. You should be in the business of arranging flowers."

From that day on Bob was doomed to be a floral designer. He couldn't escape his destiny. I've always been thankful that *I* wasn't asked to pick that bouquet and thus escaped that terrible fate.

Homelife Vignette

We ate a lot of corn in sweet-corn season. We grew acres of it, so it wasn't something we had to buy. When Mom would bring the heaped up, steaming platter to the table, everyone would cry, "Corn again!"—Our whole family was "corn-again" Christians.

Judicial Decision

A fellow seeking recreation, exercise, and pleasure decided to take up roller skating. As he tried to master the spinning wheels, however, he found that they more often mastered him, and he constantly lurched while skating. After several attempts to improve his skills, he gave up skating, as he decided that it was unconstitutional—there was no separation of *lurch* and *skate*.

Words of Wisdom and Advice to Young Friends
(On choosing a used car or a wife.)

1. First of all, be sure to choose a model that suits your situation and life-style. If your taste runs to sport's models, then lay off the family-style chassis and vice versa. Features to be found in the latter are seldom found in a topless model.
2. Economy: Forget it. You are not likely to get it in either of the above. If this is really your bag, choose a bicycle instead.

3. Check the body carefully to determine if blemishes or defects are being concealed by touch-up paint or other deceitful practices.
4. Be sure you get genuine parts; a naive or uninitiated person can be easily fooled by inferior materials, cheap replacements, or imitations.
5. Always presume that the speedometer has been turned back. For a more accurate evaluation, look for unusual amounts of wear on moving parts and areas of human contact. (It should be noted that high total mileage is not an automatic cause to reject a choice, if regular lubrication and servicing have taken place.)
6. If you have a knowlegable and experienced *older* friend, have him check out your choice thoroughly, including a trial run . . .

Crisis Communiqué

(An emergency letter, copies to each of my four sons.)

Please could you look in the part of your wardrobe that you took home last Thanksgiving or Christmas to see if you, by chance, have a pair (new) of light pants with a gold stripe in it? They *were* hanging on the pole in the dining room to be ironed a little then to be worn in the spring. Now I can't find them anyplace, so I'm hoping one of you got them by mistake. If not, I'm in a pantsless situation that is barely tolerable. I appreciate it.
So unless you've named me "Running Bare"
Please find my pants and send them there:
R.W. Groves
5 Bottomless Blvd.
Otego, N.Y. 13825
I love you guys with my heart and soul
Our family ties reach from pole to pole

And I'll give you my shirt with never a whine
But I just can't see you in pant-o-mine.
Please look! If no pants arrive by mail, I'll know you didn't find them and I'll be the em-bare-assed one.
Love,
Dad

Wedding Vows*

"I am willing to accept this woman as a member of my harem as long as she stay in tent."
—Sheik of Araby

❈ ❈ ❈ ❈

"I intend to stay with this man and accept his favors, gifts, and paycheck until I find I can do better."
—Standard female statement

❈ ❈ ❈ ❈

"I am willing to include this lady among those I love until such time as she makes my life so miserable as to be unbearable. At which time I shall split."
—Standard male version

❈ ❈ ❈ ❈

"I don't intend to recite any statement of intent 'cause I intend to do whatever I please."
—Either gender

*Given the modern trend toward writing one's own wedding vows in lieu of traditional ceremony and language, these are a few suggested samples of statements of intent.

"I intend to love you within an inch of your life, so brace yourself, Baby."

—No signature, she knows who

Pessimist's Minisermon

> Ask and you will receive. Seek and you shall find. knock and the door will be opened to you. For everyone who asks will receive and he who seeks will find, and the door will be opened to him who knocks.
>
> —Matthew 7:7–8

This is not to say you will receive that for which you ask. It may be that you will receive the direct opposite, a substitute, an excuse or an alibi, a refusal, a denial, or a punch in the nose.

Seek? Yea, verily, and you may find disappointment, disillusionment, frustration, and despair, or other problems with no easy answers.

Knock and a door will open—and you may be bowled over by the impact; yanked inside to be robbed, mugged, or raped; thrown from the premises by someone who did not wish to be disturbed; or you might find yourself at the mercy of a man-eating tiger or a man-hating woman.

Yet we must go on—asking, seeking, knocking—always hoping to find the end of the rainbow, the winning ticket, the jackpot, peace, contentment, happiness, satisfaction, et cetera. What else is life about?

> Man never was but always to be blest.
> —Alexander Pope
> "An Essay on Man," Epistle I

Grains of Truth: The Gleanings of a Lifetime

> *Any endeavor is bound to be successful if you start at the bottom and work your way up.*

Definitely true. Note that it works in nature. (Example: The way a woodchuck starts at the bottom when he digs a burrow.) Or . . .
> *Use your head.*

It always works for the woodpecker.

* * * *

> *Nudity is immoral, unnatural, indecent.*

If God had wanted us to go 'round naked, He would have had us born that way.

* * * *

Experience is one of the most valuable by-products of living and is a very precious commodity.
The reason wool is warmer than cotton is because wool has had the experience of keeping a sheep warm.

* * * *

My claim to being an efficiency expert: I use a tablespoon instead of a teaspoon while having my morning cereal. My claim to being a leader: It is founded on simply getting there *ahead* of the rest of them.

* * * *

There are two sexes—positive and negative.
Figure out which one you are not and then you will know—you are something else.

✳ ✳ ✳ ✳

Herewith a conversation between two semi-intelligent people:
"Never say, 'I'm positive,' Only a jackass is positive."
"Are you sure?"
"I'm positive."

✳ ✳ ✳ ✳

And a serious note; words of wisdom from my Grandfather Groves: "Always do more than you have to. One who does only what one must is a slave. As soon as one does more, one can do as one pleases and hence is free."

Excerpts from Groves's Laws*

It's my opinion that nobody wants to hear my opinion.

※ ※ ※ ※

Birthdays don't worry me. I notice that every time I'm a year older so is everyone else.

※ ※ ※ ※

Beautiful flowers are like beautiful women in that you don't have to own them to enjoy them.

※ ※ ※ ※

Theory of relativity: If you live halfway to Florida, your relatives will find you.

※ ※ ※ ※

Old age is the time of life when the pains are coming closer together, but no childbirth is involved.

※ ※ ※ ※

Indomitable spirit department: "He beat me every game, even though I'm the better player."
—Grandson Hank Aaron Groves, an eleven-year-old
　　　　　　　　　　　　　　　　　　　Ping-Pong player

※ ※ ※ ※

*These are the author's except where credit is given.

The reason a prophet is "without honor is his own hometown" is probably because people have heard what his wife says about him.

* * * *

On seeing a tv program based on the terrible disadvantages of being attractive or beautiful: "If you think being beautiful is so tough, just try ugly for a while."

* * * *

If things can get this fouled up here on earth, can Heaven be all *that* perfect?

* * * *

Sometimes when a person has something on his or her mind, it's best to keep it under one's hat.

* * * *

To sing in a chorus means—putting your music where your mouth is.

* * * *

Often, even when a major success eludes us, there are noteworthy minor successes. For example: A woman who tried throughout a lifetime to achieve perfectly flaky pie crusts has, herself, become flaky.

* * * *

Train a dog to come when you call him, then bang him on the head with a stick or a newspaper and he will soon learn not to come when called. Husbands are like that too, but they learn slower.

✳ ✳ ✳ ✳

When a self-made man is called to meet his maker, what a terrible confrontation!

✳ ✳ ✳ ✳

Can di-verticulosis be an illness caused by not spending enough time in the horizontal position?

✳ ✳ ✳ ✳

"A father of a large family needs to be very strong-minded; he is called a fool so often, he might otherwise start to believe it."
    —From my dad, R. W. Groves, Sr., father of eight

✳ ✳ ✳ ✳

"All things will come to he who waits." But if he has a wife who wants it, he'll get it a lot quicker.

✳ ✳ ✳ ✳

Some of us would like to see ethnic and racial bigotry and discrimination wiped out in our lifetime, but we don't stand a Chinaman's chance.

✳ ✳ ✳ ✳

It's difficult to have a great father-son relationship when both persons are highly overqualified for their roles in the situation.

* * * *

"When you feel yourself becoming depressed or despondent, do something for somebody else quick!"
—From my mom, Bertha E. Groves

* * * *

If Heaven is so wonderful, why do we go to such pains to postpone our arrival there?

* * * *

Twenty below zero: "These are the times that try men's souls" (Thomas Paine)—and their furnaces and automobile batteries.

* * * *

Having a one-track mind is forgivable—as long as it's not narrow guage.

* * * *

Reasonably logical: A composer who no longer composes must just decompose.

* * * *

On nudity: A bird's nest is never more completely exposed than when the leaves fall.

✻ ✻ ✻ ✻

A fool and his money are soon married.

✻ ✻ ✻ ✻

On the joy of motorcycling: A bird that is used to building a nest on a swinging bough will never be happy with one on a brick wall. Or . . . If you're the type of person who likes to take the curves and corners of life on two wheels, you'll be better off with a motorcycle or bicycle than with a car.

✻ ✻ ✻ ✻

Old Chinese proverb (update by RWG): 'Tis a far better thing to work one's butt off than to have an unhappy wife.

✻ ✻ ✻ ✻

Theatrical observation: If you can get a spot in a show when the audience has been sitting for about an hour and forty-five minutes, there's a good chance you'll get a standing ovation.

✻ ✻ ✻ ✻

When people become impatient because I haven't made a decision, they fail to recognize that *not* making a decision *is* making a decision.

✻ ✻ ✻ ✻

It's great if your wife thinks you're perfect, but the tough part is trying to live up to it.

❉   ❉   ❉   ❉

"A picture is worth a thousand words"—but not if you can make the words rhyme.

About the Author

Raymond W. Groves was born to a pioneering family in Northern Wisconsin on April 28, 1917, fifth in a family of eight children. At age ten, he and his family left their thriving dairy farm to move to a farm in the Susquehanna River Valley near Oneonta, New York, where they raised high-quality popcorn, sweet corn, potatoes, and small grains. After graduating from high school in the midst of the Great Depression, he served in the army during World War II and emerged to become a postal worker, moving up from carrier to supervisor in a career that lasted thirty-five years. First a father of four sons, the author is now the proud grandfather of nine children, while a late-in-life second marriage has added four families and eight more grandchildren to the fold. His poetic topics reflect the variety of his interests, which range from the Boy Scouts of America to the Red Cross blood-donor program to the Literacy Volunteer Program, as well as a host of others.